Major Edward Moor (1771-1848) was profe
A specialist in Hindu mythology, he was author of the ~~Hindu~~ ~~~
nine other books including a dictionary of Suffolk. He was the owner of Great Bealings House in Suffolk where the mysterious bell ringing described in Bealings Bells took place in 1834 and following his experiences went on to research many similar accounts from around the British Isles.

Alan Murdie is Chairman of the Ghost Club and a council member of the Society for Psychical Research. He has investigated many cases of ghost and poltergeist phenomena both in Britain and abroad. He is co-author of the 'Cambridge Ghost Book' (2000) and has written and broadcast extensively on paranormal topics

Mark Stewart-Jones is the series editor for the Ghosts Of The Ghost Club project. He has written for The Independent amongst others and is the author of two novels.

Compiled by Ivor S. Jones
Edited by Mark Stewart-Jones
Ghosts Of The Ghost Club 2000
Ghosts Of The Ghost Club 2001

By Mark Stewart-Jones
Fiction
Martin Bonehouse (1996)
An Ecstasy Of Fumbling (1998)

Non-Fiction
Sophie – Too Full Of Heaven (2000)

Bealings Bells

NEW EDITION

Major Edward Moor

Introduction and Afterword
by Alan Murdie
Chairman of The Ghost Club

Edited by Mark Stewart-Jones

The Ghost Club
London

First published as *'Bealings Bells. An Account of the Mysterious Ringing of Bells, At Great Bealings in 1834; and in other parts of England: with relations of farther unaccountable occurrences in various places'* by John Loder, Wodbridge 1841

This Edition first published by The Ghost Club 2004

This book is sold subject to the condition that it shall not, by way of trade or otherwise be lent, re-sold, hired out, photocopied or held in any retrieval system or otherwise circulated without the publishers prior consent in any form of binding or cover other than that in which it is published and without a similar condition including this condition being imposed on the subsequent purchaser.

The Ghost Club
PO Box 160
St Leonards On Sea
England
TN38 8WA

www.ghostclub.org.uk

© The Ghost Club 2004

ISBN 0-9538662-3-8

ACKNOWLEDGEMENTS

With thanks to

Stewart Evans
For allowing access and copying of
his original edition of Bealings Bells.

Dennis Bardens
(1911-2004)
For assistance in locating early references
to the book.

CONTENTS

Introduction by Alan Murdie	ix
PREFACE TO BEALINGS BELLS	17
BEALINGS BELLS	23
Afterword by Alan Murdie	111
Ghosts Of The Ghost Club	125
The Ghost Club	126

Title Page of first edition 1841

BEALINGS BELLS.

AN ACCOUNT
OF THE
MYSTERIOUS RINGING OF BELLS,
AT
GREAT BEALINGS, SUFFOLK,

IN 1834;

AND IN OTHER PARTS OF ENGLAND:

WITH RELATIONS OF FARTHER

UNACCOUNTABLE OCCURRENCES,

IN

VARIOUS PLACES:

BY

MAJOR EDWARD MOOR,
F.R.S. &c.

Woodbridge:

PRINTED AND SOLD BY JOHN LODER,
For the Benefit of the New Church.

1841.

AN INTRODUCTION TO BEALINGS BELLS
By Alan Murdie

For over half a century copies of *Bealings Bells* have been virtually unobtainable. Only a small number survive in libraries and archives and almost none are in the hands of private collectors. Yet this small book *'Bealings Bells An Account of the Mysterious Ringing of Bells, At Great Bealings in 1834; and in other parts of England: with relations of farther unaccountable occurrences in various places'* to give its full title, is one of the classics of early psychical research. As Major Edward Moor the author and principal witness to the Bealings phenomena realised, his small book represented, "probably, the greatest number of *authenticated* instances of preternatural appearances, that have hitherto been offered to public notice". What he did not realise was the fact that he had succeeded in publishing the first work devoted to poltergeist phenomena in English. However, although a lover of words and languages it seems probable that Major Moor never knew the word at all, since the word "poltergeist" itself was not to enter the language from the German for another seven years, first appearing in 1848, the year in which Moor died.[1]

The rarity of the first edition of *Bealings Bells* has led to the events described in it being only known from secondary sources by later generations of psychical researchers. Originally published in 1841, *Bealings Bells* may be described as a book very much before its time in its approach and ideas, appearing 20 years before the founding of the Ghost Club and some 40 years before the foundation of the Society for Psychical Research in 1882. Although in its early years, the Society for Psychical Research (SPR) was most active in collecting reports of apparitions there was relatively little in the way of practical investigation or what has become known as "ghost hunting". In particular the early SPR tended to be rather dismissive of reports of poltergeist cases, despite their similarity to many alleged séance room phenomena. Indeed, it was not for nearly 90 years that the book received any serious attention from scholars and researchers.

The first writer to give the Bealings Bells case serious notice was a collector of curiosities rather than a psychical researcher, Commander R.T. Gould who devoted a chapter to *Bealings Bells* in his book *More Enigmas* (1929). Commander Gould (who was later to write the first book on the Loch Ness "Monster") stated "Nowadays, those who are well-read in such matters would probably classify the Bealings Bells as a somewhat unusual but not unique, variety of the manifestation generally associated with the poltergeist".

Seven years later Harry Price – whose interest in poltergeists led him to the investigation of Borley Rectory – cited the Bealings case in his *Search for Truth* in 1936 and it attracted further notice in Sacherverall Sitwell's unusual study, *Poltergeists* (1940). Price returned to the Bealings case after World War II, devoting a chapter entitled 'Ring Out, Wild Bells' to the story in his classic *Poltergeist Over England* (1945). His interest in *Bealings Bells* was motivated both as a psychical researcher and as a rare book collector, Price being the owner of some 15000 books, now housed at the University of London library and known as the Harry Price Library.

However, despite its glowing endorsement from Price, few researchers have ever examined a copy of *Bealings Bells*. The rarity arises from the fact that Major Moor's book was a privately published volume, the proceeds of which went towards the foundation of a new church in Woodbridge. No doubt the attacks launched upon Prices's reputation and work after his death in 1948 have helped contributed to its obscurity by deterring others from re-assessing his work. A further factor encouraging obscurity was its omission from Michael Goss's Bibliography on poltergeist literature published in 1979[2] which did not include works published before 1884.

Knowledge of *Bealings Bells* and the other cases collected by Major Moor have been generally derived from Price or other secondary sources. Visits to

Great Bealings House by writers have occasionally brought researchers into contact with the book, such as Alasdair Alpin MacGregor. He included the story in his colourful collection *The Ghost Book* (1955) together with the story of a haunting of another property in the village called Rosery Cottage. MacGregor was particularly keen both on Suffolk and stories of phantom bells so the story had obvious appeal. Sixteen years later the Bealings Bells case merited an entry in Peter Underwood's influential *Gazeteer of British Ghosts* (1971) and Anthony Hippesley Cox in *Haunted Britain* (1973) on visiting Great Bealings House remarked that the bells were "now disconnected but one wonders if that would prevent another outbreak."

Marc Alexander also describes the case and book in *Phantom Britain* (1975). Thereafter references to Major Moor seem to largely disappear from ghost and poltergeist literature and many recent books tend to omit the collection altogether. A handful of Amercian writers have mentioned the case, notably Rosemary Ellen Guiley in *The Encyclopedia of Ghosts and Spirits* and parapsychologist D. Scott Rogo who made a passing reference to the Bealings Bells in his book *The Poltergeist Experience* (1979). Scott Rogo stated "....the Bealings Bells case of 1834.... illustrates not the grandeur of the poltergeist, but the poltergeist in its weakest and most puerile form" a remark which taken at face value would hardly inspire anyone to search out the original book. Indeed, his knowledge seems to have been largely derived from Commander Gould's account, although D. Scott Rogo states "Moor was no fool by any means, and didn't immediately jump to the conclusion that a ghost was loose in the house". Scott Rogo did nonetheless also include an extract from one of Moor's collected cases, although the others have received no attention to the present.

Even in Suffolk where the events took place, local knowledge of the case has faded, although a dramatised and garbled version of Bealings Bells appeared in Hugh Mills' *Ghosts of East Anglia* (1984). In this version, the story is set in summer rather than February and thus, it may be seen that 170 years after the events described the story is in danger of drifting into legend and distortion. Thus, a re-print is more than justified, since Bealings Bells is an account of a mystery that remains unsolved to this day.

On an editorial note, the structure and layout of Bealings Bells has been retained but the number of pages has altered. I have made minor alterations to certain spellings e.g "surprise" instead of "surprize" and "honour" instead of "honor" and corrected occasional misspellings in the text. The footnotes inserted are those of Major Moor unless otherwise indicated. The page numbers in the text refer to the current edition.

(1)   The first use of the word in English was by Mrs Catherine Crowe in her classic *The Night Side of Nature* (1848)

(2)   Goss, Michael in Poltergeists: An annotated Bibliography of Works in English c. 1880-1975. (1979) Scarecrow Press, 1979.

BEALINGS BELLS

Dedication Page of first edition 1841

TO

MRS. SHAWE,

OF KESGRAVE HALL,

NEAR WOODBRIDGE, SUFFOLK,

This Volume,

COMPILED AND PRINTED AT HER SUGGESTION,

IS

MOST RESPECTFULLY INSCRIBED

BY HER

AFFECTIONATE FRIEND AND NEIGHBOUR,

E.M.

GREAT BEALINGS,
August 1841.

PREFACE

Conversing with a lady in this neighbourhood – to whom this little book is inscribed – and to whose influence, *the cause* is more indebted than to anyone – on the means of augmenting the scanty funds for building the intended Church at Woodbridge, she suggested that I should cause to be printed, an account of the MYSTERIOUS BELL-RINGING at Bealings, to be sold at the intended bazaar in September.

To this I assented – and the little book in your hand, kind Reader, is the result.

As such ringings have not occurred in my house only; but have, within my knowledge, extended to others, I proceeded to make enquiry into occurrences elsewhere: and, in addition to several accounts already, then in my possession, I have been favoured with many others, which I have added, in extension of the bulk of my volume; and in augmentation, as I hope and believe, of the interest and entertainment, that it may excite and afford.

In making such collection of facts, I have been furnished with relations of circumstances, not exactly coming within the description of BELL-RINGING: still wearing similar preternatural aspects, that I have not hesitated to add them – in view to the effect indicated in the conclusion of the preceding paragraph. Some of them, as will be seen, still more extraordinary than what I have witnessed – and equally authentic.

If, within the limited extent of my knowledge and enquiry, so many instances of such things have been heard of; it is not to be doubted but in a wider circle, -say all England –very many others have occurred, not hitherto brought to public notice. Some, possibly, still more extraordinary and perhaps, so varying in their phenomena, as might, if collected, throw light on such unaccountable occurrences; and, haply, lend a clue to the discovery of their cause.

Nor is it likely that such mysterious appearances have been confined to England.

Assuming the cause to be preternatural, it is surely sufficiently curious, to warrant scientific enquiry into the origin of such extraordinary phenomena. Such enquiry is beyond my power to carry out.

Had the mysterious ringing been confined to that of my own house, my conviction of the cause assumed would have been sufficiently strong. But strengthened as it is, by still more extraordinary events of a like nature, as related in the following pages, I confidently expect that a like conviction will be wrought in the minds of a great majority of those who may read this little volume. It contains probably, the greatest number of authenticated instances of preternatural appearances, that have hitherto been offered to public notice.

The author, or compiler, has, in the currency of this work, indulged in some occasional remarks; which may tend to lessen the necessity of any lengthened introductory matter.

Some of the communications may have a tendency to throw over the whole an air of incredulity; or even ridicule. If it be so, the author cares not. He has no hypothesis to uphold. He has honestly related what he has seen, and heard. He has invented nothing: nor withheld anything, likely to throw light on the obscurity of his subject.

I need scarcely add, that I shall hear, with much interest, of any attempt, by competent persons, to unravel the mysteries herein made known.

And that I shall thankfully receive any authenticated relation of similar occurrences, not in my possession. In the event of a reprint of my book, I shall gladly introduce them.

If, indeed, the whole of what is here related be a trick, as some, not having seen, may be disposed to think – and I can scarcely blame any such, for so thinking –if, I say, it is trickery- the performers, be they who they may, possess a knowledge, a power, hitherto, unattained by science.

When the following pages were all nearly printed, I mentioned their subject to my old friend and kind neighbour BERNARD BARTON; of whose poetical effusions, his county-men are so justly proud; hinting my hope of something introductory, from his ready pen.

My sheets were sent – and speedily acknowledged and returned with the following note:

DEAR MAJOR, - Thy pacquet is duly received, and is now in Lucy's hands; this evening I hope to read it myself; and, after having done so, to write, or, to may be, rhyme, thereon;

> But how the subject theme may gang,
> Let time and chance determine;
> Perhaps it may turn out a sang
> Perhaps turn out a sermon

So sang Robin Burns, and so say , for I can at present form no conjecture what aspect the theme may wear on laying down thy leaves; only I know I should like to have a "finger in the pie". But do not look for any thing very clear: the case is full of ambiguity and mystery. Poetry seldom clears up such: -rather tends to make them more mysterious, by its veil of gossamer. Besides the crying folly of this utilitarian age, is to have every thing made clear: it is in harmony with its superficial impertinence to decry all mystery: to want to have everything proved by demonstration, and clearly accounted for, on philosophical principles. I have small sympathy with such shallow philosophy, and am always glad when anything, however trivial, occurs, which makes such would-be knowing ones at fault. If I knew how thy bells were rung, methinks I would not tell every one: though I should like to be able to gratify thy own *rational* curiosity. However, I am well content it should still remain a mystery. It is far more poetical, than if it were cleared up. Then the odds are, there would be little in it. Now there is somewhat, though not perhaps much beyond it being incomprehensible; and that is something nowadays.

What I may write, be it introductory or valedictory, or both, I will put my name to, with thy leave; that I may not comprise thee, or anyone else, by any view I take of the subject. And now farewell.

B.B.

WOODBRIDGE 6 mo. 22, 1841
   Noon.

P.S. Evening. Since writing the above I have indited six "introductory," and seven "Valedictory" stanzas: which I place at thy disposal.

Do not take fright at the opening stanzas of the Introductory ditty, but read on, in the faith that thy Poet is not one of the *Praters* – whose words he has put in inverted commas, to denote that they are not his own. My own favourite, of the two Pieces, is the "Valedictory" one, because it gave me an opportunity of saying my say, as far as time, space, and subject allowed, on the cold, calculating, sceptical philosophy of this utilitarian age. We are getting as hard as nether mill-stone – as dry as "the remainder biscuit after a voyage:" like old Cutting of Playford who used to boast he believed nothing that he heard, and only half of what he saw. I hold not with the Cutting-onian Philosophy, but am always willing to take marvels on trust, when reported by a lover of truth like thyself.

B.B.

These stanzas – in our Poet's usual beautiful style of versification, I most gladly give, in their appropriate places:- having, now, more confidence in the fair reception of a book, which begins and ends so well.

Bespeaking the indulgent Reader's unprejudiced consideration – a perusal of the following pages is respectfully invited.

EDWARD MOOR.

Great Bealings
Near Woodbridge, Suffolk
15th *August,* 1841

Introductory verses from first edition 1841

INTRODUCTORY VERSES.

"A Book about those Bealings Bells!
"What can be more absurd?
"The thing—whate'er the Major tells,
"Was *trickery*, on my word!

"'Twas but a quiz; a clever hoax.
"Play'd by some lad, or lass;
"Or both, perhaps; and wiser folks
"As such, had let it pass."

Thus, peradventure, some may prate :—
Reader; with courteous grace,
Ere thou shalt give thy judgement, wait
'Till thou hast read the case.

A plain straight-forward tale it tells;
And proves, from various sources,
Not THESE *alone*, but OTHER Bells
Have run their random courses.

Who rang them; or the reason why
They rung at all—believe
We have no favourite theory,
Whose fall can make us grieve.

Facts—simple facts alone, we state;
We've studied them in vain;
And having stated them, we wait,
'Till you their cause explain.

BERNARD BARTON.

No 1.

To the Editor of the Ipswich Journal

Sir,- A circumstance of an unaccountable nature has recently occurred in my house, and I shall be obliged by your giving insertion to this, my account of it. It commenced on Sunday, the 2nd inst.; and on the Tuesday and Wednesday and Thursday following, I drew up an account of it, intended for your paper; but my account was so long that I could scarcely expect, curious as I deemed it, that you could spare room. But having had many enquiries into the circumstances, and having seen in a newspaper an imperfect and erroneous statement, I am induced to send you an abridged account, from my minutes made at the time. On Sunday, the 2nd inst. returning from afternoon service, I was told that the dining-room bell has been rung three times, at intervals, between two and five o'clock. At this, the servants left in the house, a man and woman, were surprised; but no person or cause being perceptible, though sought. This passed; and had nothing more happened, would probably have been soon forgotten. The next day, Monday, the same bell rang three or four times in the afternoon- the last time within my hearing, shortly before five P.M.. This too might have passed; for I fancied I could discern a cause sufficient for such an effect, although the room was not in use, and certainly no one was within reach of the bell-pull: but the proceedings of yesterday (Tuesday, the 4th) have, I confess completely baffled me. I left home early, and returned before five in the afternoon. I was immediately told that "all the bells in the kitchen had been ringing violently." A *peal* at that moment sounded in my ears. I proceeded thither, and learned from the cook, that "the five bells on the right" had, since about three o'clock, been frequently so affected. There are nine bells in a row, about a foot apart, 10 feet from the floor, and 12 feet from the fire; not over it. While I was intently looking at the bells, and listening to the relation that the ringings had occurred at intervals of about a quarter of an hour, the same five bells rang violently; so violent was it that I should not have been surprised if they had been shaken from their fastenings. My son was beside me, also watching: he had witnessed one peal before, and had heard more than one. The cook and another servant were then in the kitchen. Although expecting a ringing, the suddenness and violence of the effect, with the agitation of the bells, rather startled me. My son said he had been startled by the first witnessed-peal; so had the cook, but she had heard and seen so many that she was now unmoved. After about 10 minutes, I intently watching the while, another similar phenomena was witnessed; but we thought not quite so loud as that preceding, and we were in some doubt if more than four bells actually rung. With an accession of observers, we continued watching during about another quarter of an hour, when a third peal, by the five, occurred; very like those preceding, but some of us thought less loud. [In my original letter to you here followed an account of how the bells are hung, the origin, conducting, and termination, of the wires; but it is long, and I omit it; although in an investigation of the cause of what I am describing I should deem such particulars necessary.] The five bells, whose pealing I have mentioned, are those of the dining-room, drawing-room over it, an adjacent bedroom – neither of these rooms is in use- and two attics over the drawing-room.

We arrived at the time before 6, of Tuesday, the 4th. Dinner was taken in the "breakfast room" (some call it the "library"); when sitting down, the bell of that room rang singly, as if it had been pulled; no one was near the pull; it having rung after we sat down to dinner. During dinner the same five bells rang, perhaps 10,12, or 15 minutes – on recollection, I think oftener, say four times - and continued to do so, with nearly uniform violence, while the servants, six in number, were at dinner in the kitchen; and, with longer intervals, till ¼ before 8, when the last peal of Tuesday sounded. During our dinner we thought one peal did not sound so clear as the other clangings, and in notes differing from their usual tone: such, it was remarked, as are sometimes heard from a dull copper sheep-bell. I afterwards learned that the dull peal was noticed in the kitchen, and proceeded from the *three* bells on the left of the nine. These three pealed but that once; they are of the room where we dined, of a bed-room near it, and a bed-room adjoining the last; all in use. Here ended the Tuesday ringing, except one gentle sounding of a bell, about an hour after the last peal, hung by itself on the side of the kitchen, opposite the nine; to that bell the wire leads from an attic.

The nine bells have been hung for 28 years, and so well hung that they have never, I think, required any repair, save that of the breakfast-room; the wire of which broke, and was repaired a month or six weeks ago by a tradesman of Woodbridge, who assisted at the original hanging. All the bells in the house - 12 in number- except one, have thus rung, without apparent cause. The one is the front door bell which hangs between the five *pealers* and the three. It is the largest and loudest, and has hitherto preserved its gravity and taciturnity.

Now, Sir, is this not a strange relation ? At the first gentle, single, tinkling, I was disposed to think that I could account for it. [I omit my theory, as the former omission of the currency of the wires would render it unintelligible.] But the boisterous clang and agitation of my first witnessed peal of five, at once showed its fallacy. You and your readers may be assured that there is no hoax in the matter. I do not mean by me, but by any one. I am thoroughly convinced that the ringing is by no human agency. How then is it ? I cannot say. A satisfactory solution is beyond the reach of my philosophy. [The preceding was written when my curiosity was on the stretch, and my feeling excited to a high pitch of amusement. A lapse of several weeks and due reflection do not induce me to weaken the force of the expression.] At *this moment*, 11 A.M., on Wednesday, the 5th comes a peal. I, my son, and grandson, in the breakfast room; enter a reporter- it was of the original peal of five, of usual violence- three or four persons in the kitchen - *at this instant*, an interval of three minutes, comes another peal, like the last. I go to the kitchen. I return and note that three minutes after, I intently looking, the five rung very violently; again in 4 minutes, more violently than ever. One actually struck against the ceiling: that is, the spiral flexible iron on which it is hung, so struck. This was the right hand bell, of the best bedroom. In 2 minutes more, another peal of 5, less violent than the last. At this peal the cook started and exclaimed, Oh! 4 or 5 persons were now in the kitchen; one, a tradesman's servant from Woodbridge who declared "he was never so stamm'd in all his life". 3 minutes another peal of the average sort. I continued watching another quarter of an hour, but nothing further occurred. I now sent a servant round to ring all the bells singly, I noticing the effect. They sounded as usual, uninjured by their unusual treatment; their motion, when thus rung by hand, and that of their spiral flexible support, was comparatively slow and perceptible - not so at the peals - it was then too rapid to be seen distinctly.

[I now went to examine some of the wires, but omit particulars, for reasons given in former parentheses.] Returning to the kitchen, I learned that the single bell, opposite the 9, had, since the last noticed peal, rung gently and frequently; it rung, in my sight, half a minute after. The wire to this is from a bed-room. The twelfth, hitherto unnoticed, bell is in the attic, rung from a bed-room; this has rung frequently, but not violently.

I repeated that I am, baffled as to a sufficient cause of what I have thus seen, and heard, and described. The weather has been calm - nothing particular in atmospheric phenomena - barometer nearly stationary at 29 deg. - thermometers within their usual range; three are daily noticed. The known laws of the electric theory seem inadequate in their ordinary operation - as are those of the expansion of metals by change of temperature.

I am now, near noon of Wednesday, the 5th called to Woodbridge. - 5 p.m., I now return. The peals of five are reported to me to have continued after I left. The first, half an hour after; and four others succeeded with nearly like intervals - the last about half-past 2. The single bell opposite tinkled two or three times, and was observed to shake as often, without ringing. The bell in the attic also rang several times, gently. Thursday,10 A.M. Nothing farther has occurred in the ringing way since the afternoon, as mentioned, of yesterday. We expect no more. If any thing further should occur, I may trouble you again briefly.

I think, Sir, this strange relation will amuse you and your readers. And if you or any of them can give a satisfactory explanation for it, I farther think it will be instructive to many – and among them to your very obedient Servant,

EDWARD MOOR

Bealings, 25th Feb. 1834.

P.S. I had on the above date an opportunity of reading the above proceedings up to that time, to six or eight very intelligent gentlemen at Woodbridge – and add, as my answer to some of their queries- that I keep no monkey -that my house is not infested by rats – that the wires of the five, and of the three, peelers, are visible in their whole course, from their pull to the bells, save where they go through the walls, in which the holes seem no bigger than is necessary. The wires of the two single bells are also visible, except where they go through floors or walls. One or two of my friends, said it was *"all a trick"*. *It is possible.* I have for many years of my life passed over large arcs of the earth's surface, and have seen divers tricks of distant people. If this be one, it surpasses all that I have seen. I have heard of things something alike – that is of strange ringing of bells – formerly and recently in Woodbridge, and in your good town of Ipswich: but not the particulars. I mean to try some experiments, if I can, on metallic expansion- the atmosphere is beyond my reach. The preceding is, except when otherwise indicated, merely a transcription from my longer letter of the 5th. I am now – the 27th – able to add that nothing particular has since occurred. I have read this account to persons who heard and saw, most of what I heard and saw; and some proceedings that I did not. They concur in the opinion that it is a fair and unembellished statement of the facts.

Bealings, 27th February, 1834

The preceding appeared in the *Ipswich Journal*, of 1st March , 1834. And in the paper of that day fortnight - 15th March - the following Letter appeared - which I call No. 2. I consider what will hereafter appear - though not prepared as any sort of reply to No.2 - sufficient thereon. Adding, merely, that I did not in any way, follow the advice therein offered.

No.2.

To the Editor of the Ipswich Journal.

SIR, - I do not flatter myself that I am able to elucidate the mystery of the bell-ringing, at Mr Moor's of Bealings, but I beg to offer a suggestion to that gentleman, and if he follow it, I will make him any moderate wager, that he shall either discover the cause of the ringing, or that the bells will not ring at all during any part of the time, however long, that he may be pursuing the investigation. My plan is this, - when Mr. Moor is favoured with a repetition of the mysterious peal, I recommend him, instead of watching for monkeys or cats, or making philosophical experiments, to send for a few respectable neighbours - seat his entire establishment in one room, and leave a friend with them - lock all the outer doors of the house and take the keys - station a friend on each stair-case, and with another friend make a thorough search of the house, locking every door, and taking out the key as the search proceeds. If this plan be pursued I will, as above mentioned, make any moderate bet, either that the bells will not ring at all during the search, or that, if they do ring, the party searching will find some relative, or friend, of one of his establishment concealed in some part of the house.

In my house, which compared with Mr. Moor's, is of limited extent, a person may, in a second, set three bells ringing violently by touching the wires, which all pass along the passage and through a whole in the wall, and in less than two seconds may enter the kitchen in a different direction from that of the passage where the three bells were set ringing.

Mr. Moor does not say whether the wires of the five bells all pass through one hole into the kitchen, and the wires of the three bells through another, but I take it for granted such is that fact; and if so, of course, it gives great facility to the party to play the foolish trick upon the family. Probably the wire of the front door bell does not hang conveniently to be touched in hastily passing it, which may account for the silence of that bell on these mysterious occasions.

I have heard of many nearly similar tricks of noises, &c. about a house, one of which I will relate: it was in a farm house in a parish very little distant from Bealings: a great variety of tricks were played for several weeks, and it was currently reported, either that the house must be haunted, or that the mistress of the house, a very infirm superannuated woman, was bewitched, and the poor old woman was cruelly treated by part of the family, in the supposition of her being the cause of the mysterious proceedings. Amongst other neighbours consulted on the occasion was my poor mother, to whom the master of the house said, "would you believe, Mrs _____-, that my wife could be such a wicked hypocrite as to pretend she cannot get up and down stairs without being carried, and yet do all this mischief in the house - she must be bewitched." My poor mother, though no conjurer, had no inconsiderable share of that useful, though somewhat rare, article, vulgarly called common sense, replied, "bewitched or not bewitched, your poor wife has nothing to do with these proceedings - watch your servants, particularly the girl allotted to you from H— Workhouse, and you will soon find out who is bewitched." – The advice was followed – the girl was suspected and dismissed, having obtained the appellation of "Mischieful" which I have heard she retained when she soon after appeared on the *pave* in Ipswich.

A CONSTANT READER

Hadleigh, March 3rd, 1834.

What precedes in No.1. is the substance of our observances of the phenomena under our notice; but not the sum. It is noted above – parenthetically – that, considering the length of my letter to the Editor of the Ipswich Journal, I had omitted some passages, that I had intended to send.

Those passages I will now give: being less restricted as to room: - with some additions.

"Let me here explain how these five bells are situated. I conceive it necessary for the discovery of the cause of these strange effects. The bell which first rung, on the Sunday, is that of the dining room. It has two horizontal pulls, by brass buttons; one on each side of the fire-place. The wires are led from the pulls, through the projecting pierced jambs and walls, a distance of 3 feet. To the outside of the western end of this house. The house fronts as nearly true south, as may be. The wires on reaching the outside, are fastened, in the usual way, to perpendicular cranks. The southern, or left hand wire as you face the fire-place, is led up perpendicularly 10 feet, and then makes a right angle, by being turned on a horizontal crank to the north. After so running 12 feet, it is again turned, by another horizontal crank, in a right angle, into another pierced hole, or aperture, again into the house. This, I shall call a common aperture; it being such to all the wires, now under consideration. Between the two dining-room brass bell-pulls, is 5 feet.

The right-hand, or northern wire, runs, like the other, through the pierced jamb and western end wall of the house; and there, by a perpendicular crank, is turned upwards to the common aperture. These two wires are joined near the aperture; and are led into it by one horizontal crank.

Before we trace the dining-room bell wire any farther, we will bring the wires of the room over it, called the drawing room; to the same point – (also the wires of the attic bed-rooms) – the common aperture.

Those of the drawing-room are on each side the fire-place – pulled by brass knobs, or buttons, like those of the dining room: and at the outside of the house, are, in like manner, fixed to perpendicular cranks – and led downwards, about 6 feet; near to the ascending wires of the dining room. Thence – by horizontal cranks – they are led to the common aperture: parallel, and close, to the wires of the dining-room – being previously joined or twisted together – near the common aperture; into which the joined wire is turned by one horizontal crank.

The "best bedroom" is on the same floor as the drawing-room – having a brick wall between. The bell-pull is a silken tassel and cord about 9 feet long; pendant from a crank near the ceiling; which crank has the wire at its other end. It is led – west – along the ceiling, about 6 feet, to another crank, near the corner of the room; where a third, turns it perpendicularly downward, a foot, to another – which turns it horizontally through a hole in the western end wall of the house. It is there, outside, turned southward, a few inches, to the common aperture. To that point, this bed-room wire, is thus led, turned by one perpendicular, and four horizontal cranks.

This is a tedious – and, it may be thought, an unnecessary detail. But I shall endeavour to show presently that it is not unnecessary. I will not make it more tedious, by following the attic wires so minutely: noting only, that after divers perpendicular and horizontal turnings, by cranks, they are led from the rooms to the common external aperture.

We have now brought the five wires to the common aperture, at the west end of the house. And here seems the time to note that all over that end as far as the wires are concerned, is spread, trained, and nailed, an old, full-wooded, pear tree; between which and the red brick end of the house, the wires are led, close to the bricks.

Five horizontal cranks with as many wires, turn in the common aperture, which is pierced through the western end wall, into a back-house on the ground floor; divided from the dining-room by a thick brick wall. It is 17 feet wide, in the direction of the wires – that is from west to east.

The five wires run straight, parallel, and close together, under the ceiling, to the corner opposite the aforesaid common aperture. There they are fixed to, and turned by, as many cranks, at a right angle, 7 feet, northerly. They are then turned east, by five other cranks, at a right angle, into and through a second common aperture, in a brick wall fourteen inches thick, into a passage.

The passage is eighteen feet long, connecting the back-house and the kitchen – having the back-house door at one end, and a kitchen window, occupying the whole width of the passage, at the other.

The passage is partly open to the external air; and is very light : so that anything that may pass or be, in it, is under the ready inspection of any one in the kitchen.

About the middle of the passage, another wire, that of the front door bell – joins company with the aforesaid five. And they run together to, and through, a third common aperture, into the kitchen, over the window.

There – in the kitchen – they are turned, by six cranks, at a right angle, again to the north. The last named wire of the six – that of the front door – at a distance of a foot from the third common aperture, is fixed finally to its bell in the usual way. At two feet, that of the dining-room terminates, at its bell. At three feet, that of the best bed-room. At four and five feet, those of the attics – and at six feet that of the drawing-room – at their respective bells.

It has been observed, that the front door bell – the nearest to the third aperture – the heaviest of the nine – did not sound at all. It will be not further noticed. Those on its right, to the north, are those, and especially the four on the right, that have played the pranks under description.

But, I repeat, all this may have little or nothing to do with the facts witnessed. The bells rang scores of times when no one was in the passage, or back-house, or house, or grounds unseen. I have waited in the kitchen, for a repetition of the ringings, with all the servants present – when no one hardly "so much as a mouse" – could be in concealment. But what matters ? – neither I, nor the servants – singly or together – nor any one – be he whom he may, could or can, I aver, work the wonderment, that I, and more than half a score others, saw.

The mention of "a mouse," reminds me of a little anecdote. I had – after the publication of the preceding letter No.1 – been occasionally requested, by neighbours and friend to tell the story of my bell-ringings. And once by a lady at Bury – an old friend. I did so; to her and another lady present – her friend – thinking to communicate some of my own mysterious feeling to my fair auditors. – "Surely" – said the friend – "it must have been mice." – Somewhat astounded at my failure, in effect, I could not help asking the unmoved lady, if she thought it likely, that what in observance, could astonish half a dozen tolerably intelligent persons, and affright as many more, could have been of so trivial a nature as to have come within the potency of mice to cause.

Now- I blame not those who, not having seen what I have, may feel disposed to consider what I have related, as arising from trick, or monkeys, or mice. But I will add, that had such (reasonably perhaps) incredulous persons, seen what I have, I cannot but think that they could no longer continue so. No one who witnessed the phenomena, could in my opinion, deem them the result of tricks; or but any preternatural cause.

I will now state why the minutia of horizontality, perpendicularity, and obliquity, in the course of the wires, are of some moment – in reference to the probability of our having been imposed on by a trick : and as bearing on the eventual discovery of the cause.

Let the reader imagine a person in the passage, between the backhouse door and the kitchen window, with say a boat-hook in hand – or with a string tied round the five or six parallel wires – and let the person be supposed to pull, as violently as you please, by the hook or by the string. What would be the consequence ? – Not the violent ringing of five or six bells, whose wires were so pulled. "And why not?" do you ask ? For this reason – to agitate the bells violently, you must pull in the direction of the line of wires, horizontally or perpendicularly – no matter. But your *downward* pull, however violent or gentle, you pull in a *contrary* direction: and if violently, the bells will not ring – if gently, they will tinkle gently, as in the usual way of ringing: - but by no means with the jerking violence that we witnessed,. I have at this moment tried the preceding facts with a hoe.

And, while I was so doing – two minutes ago – this 6th of March, 1841 – the servant of the Woodbridge butcher, who then supplied, and now supplied, my house with meat, passed me in the passage. Recollecting that he was one of the gazers with me, and five or six others, on the violent bells, I reminded him of it; and asked him if he could so ring them – if he had any notion of how it was done – and what he thought he had before seen? He said that he had no notion how it could be done – that he was astonished at what he saw – and feared mischief at the time.

I have mentioned in the early part of my foregoing letter, page 23 that when I was first told on the Sunday that the dining-room bell had rung unaccountably – had nothing further happened, it might have passed without much observance – for I fancied I could discern a cause sufficient for such effect.

This was the fancied cause. – All over the exterior western end of the house (of course outside of the wires which are kept by loops or little stapes close to the red brick wall) a full-wooded old pear tree is, as has been already mentioned, trained, and nailed. Adverting to the season – it struck me as *possible* – that two or three or more blackbirds, in which we abound, might have got among the boughs of the pear tree; and if fighting, or struggling, or cooing, might have tightened or shaken the wires sufficiently to tinkle a bell.

But mark – I had then seen nothing; and, on the Monday, had only heard, one tinkling, from a distance.

After what I saw heard, not all the blackbirds in existence, could, in my conviction, have produced such effects.

I will here, note, once for all – that after much consideration, I cannot reach any procedure by which they have been, or can be, produced.

If I had a year to devote to such considerations, and the promise of a thousand pounds in the event of discovery, I should despair of success. I would not, indeed, attempt it.

There is a point, from which all the five ringers could be set in simultaneous motion. Which point is – in a line opposite to the first named common aperture. A rope led horizontally, fixed somehow to those five cranks, and so pulled would ring them. But they could not be rung with the violent jerks witnessed and described. With no vigour of pull could that be effected. The cranks and wires might be broken: and I have no doubt but they would be, with very much less violence of pull. This is the only mode that occurs to me by which I could, even gently, ring the four or five bells. I confess, however, that the ringing in the passage, by the direct downward pull, moved the whole six bells into sound, easier than I had foreseen, or expected, before trial.

But it does not shake my expressed conviction – that my bells were not so rung by mortal hand.

Seeing, however, that I could gently ring the six bells with a hoe, by a direct downward pull in the passage – rather, as I have confessed, contrary to my expectation, - I, soon after, proceeded one crank farther back – into the back-house – and pulled downward – on the 7 feet line of wires, and produced the same effect of sound. Also on the 17 feet of line, in the backhouse; beyond the third series of cranks and directions of wires, from the bells; with the gentle, tinkling, result.

The publication of the preceding letter, No.1 – in the Ipswich Journal of 1st March, 1834, brought me, soon after, the following. It is from a lady, of whom I had some previous knowledge. She is a woman of great energy and character:- and, as will be perceived, of talent; notwithstanding her tendency to superstitious feeling. I omit her name – not having permission to use it. I do not indeed, know if she is living.* – She has suffered much; and felt deeply. In her correspondence with me, on this and other occasions, she mixes up personal and domestic matters, with the more immediate subject of her letters. Such portions I have, where convenient, omitted-

I call the following letter No.3.

No.3.

_____, *SUFFOLK, March 6, 1834*

Sir, - A lady having lent me the Ipswich Journal of last week, I have perused therein a letter of your's with a particular and painful interest; for the bells in my late father's house, rang with great violence, for some months, without apparent cause; some of the circumstances of which I

---

*This was written in 1841

shall relate. I should much like to know, if you should be able to discover any cause for your bells ringing. I was the daughter and sole heir of the late ⸺ at whose decease, I came into possession of a considerable real and personal estate. I was entrapped into a marriage with ⸺ which brought me to beggary and want, save a residence, in this abode of my forefathers, under the protection of the Lord Chancellor.

My late father died in the 47th year of his age, of pulmonary consumption, in a house at ⸺ in Kent, which he had built for his own residence, about seven years before, in the most substantial manner. My mother was at the same time seized with an alarming and dangerous illness. My attention to the bells ringing without cause, was first attracted by a servant entering hastily into my mother's chamber, who stated the bell had been rung with great violence. I used to direct her to go immediately to my father's room, and generally went myself, in the first instance, to know if anything particular had occurred or was wanted, and afterwards because I found the servant so much appalled. When I mentioned to my father the circumstances of the bell-ringing without apparent cause, he seemed displeased, and said, "you will get superstitious by conversing with nurses ." He was very ill at the time, and under my then distressing circumstances very little was said about the matter.

My mother was entirely confined to her chamber; but my father changed his sitting and sleeping rooms; when a bell in the attic, and a bell which hung in the lower hall, both of which could be rung from my mother's chamber, began to ring, but they never rang at the same time. Both these bells began to ring in the month of February, the same time of year as your's, and rang more frequently in that month, but always with great violence. They continued to ring at intervals during the month of March. In the beginning of April my poor mother died; immediately after which, my father, much against my inclination, and to my surprise, announced his intention, which his physicians did not oppose, of removing into the chamber in which my mother had breathed her last; and as soon as the room had been washed and ventilated. The bed hangings and the window curtains washed, he caused himself to be carried by three men upon a blanket into this chamber, where he himself breathed his last upon the 30th of May; during all which time the bells, or more correctly, a bell, continued to ring at intervals without apparent cause, and with great violence.

One serene day in the month of June following, I was going to take a walk in the garden with a gentleman to whose care my father had consigned me ; when we were in the lower hall, just above his head, the bell rang with great violence. We stopped, and I said to him, "now I hope you will believe the bells have rung without apparent cause;" for he used to turn the matter off, and say some person must have pulled the bell, or the wire had caught; but it was then impossible for him to do otherwise than to admit a fact for which he could not account. This was the only time I ever saw the bell in its tremendous motion, which appeared sufficient to shatter it to fragments, and yet the bells were uninjured- were in perfect order, and continued so to be until I finally quitted the house, on the first of March following. After this time, in June, the bells ceased from ringing without cause. There was at that time no other person in the house, but a servant in the kitchen, the door of which from the hall was open, and she could have no communication with the bell or its wire. Besides, she herself had been appalled by the bells for months previously - had had the extra work of running up two flights of stairs in consequence; nor was there ever any person in the house who could have had any motive for wantonly ringing a bell, and particularly under all the circumstances.

To prevent the possibility of a mouse harbouring in the house, my father had caused rubbish to be rammed down, and filled up with sand, between the walls and the skirting board, &c. The bells were well hung with copper wire, and had never required any repair; and we had then resided seven years in the house after it had been built. My father was a person of great talent, and universal knowledge; and he had himself constantly inspected and spared no expense in the building. I don't think he ever heard the bell ring for himself, or he paid into particular attention; he was ill, and the room doors were thick – but I frequently heard it myself. My parents had always ordered me to ring a bell gently, and never to pull with any violence, except something particularly should occur, when it being unusual, a servant would instantly answer the bell. There was no bell to the outer door, which bell appears to be the only in your house which has not rung.

There was no cat at my father's- and at that time the bell rang in June, the dog was close beside me, capering at the thoughts of a walk in the garden.

I was not, but you are, in circumstances to investigate the matter.

I was not brought up to believe in signs or tokens; nevertheless the experience of my eventful life leads me now to think that, such things may be; and it would be presumption in man to limit the power of the Almighty. This house, like most ancient ones, was reported to be haunted; and had the bells rung here instead of my father's new-built house, it might have been a confirmation of this report.

      I have honour to be, Sir,
          Your very obedient Servant,

―――――――

From this letter, it is evident that ringings, something similar to mine, occurred in the family and house of the unfortunate lady, who wrote it. I need not add, that although I commiserate her unhappiness, and earnestly hope that, if living, it has ceased, and that if dead, she died in peace, I do not share on her imputation of the ringings to supernatural causes: or in her belief that human weal or woe was among their effects.

I will note here, that my letter in the Ipswich Journal was abridged, or in its substance given, in several papers in London, and elsewhere.

Some of them imputed the effects described to supernatural causes; and stated, or implied, that such was my belief. I found it expedient to correct such imputation, and expressly rejected sharing in such belief. In fact, one editor, at least, confounded supernatural with preternatural. And if metropolitan editors can do so, some rural readers may. In prevention, therefore, of such misapprehension, I may be pardoned if I give the meanings of those words from Johnson's Dictionary: -

Preternatural Differing from what is natural. Irregular, in a manner different from the common order of nature.
Supernatural. Being above the order of nature. Above the cause, or power of nature.

It appears that I wrote an early answer to the letter No.3 - for I soon received another from the same lady - of which the following is a copy - with the omission of certain passages, as before.

No.4.

_____ , *SUFFOLK, March 28, 1834*

Sir, - I beg leave to return you my best thanks for the honour and favour of your letter upon the subject of bell-ringing without apparent cause; and as I am deeply interested about the matter, and anxious for an investigation into the cause, if any can be discovered, and as you are in town and can converse with scientific men, I am induced to state some further particulars to you. I regret that at the time I could not muster courage enough to state the circumstances to the late Sir Humphrey Davy, to whom I was introduced, and attended the lectures at the Royal Institution in Albermarle-street, the season after the decease of my parents.

The late Dr. Babington was one of the physicians who attended my father. Soon after my parents' decease, when I was staying with Mrs. Opie, in the house of her late father, Dr Alderson, of Norwich, I mentioned the matter to the Doctor; but he, as well as Mrs Opie and others, thought it trick, or fancy, and that it was superstitious to connect it in any way with the death of my parents; and I was deterred from mentioning the matter, until the perusal of your letter in the Ipswich Journal (which I most heartily thank you for writing) induced me to write to you upon the subject.

After what I had experienced myself, when I was a young girl, I was not so much surprised to find a writer in the Ipswich Journal, attribute the bell-ringing in your house entirely to trick; but I wish he could hear such sounds as I have done. As to the conceit, of your servants having some friend concealed in the house; would not a person in such circumstances be more likely to remain quiet than to sound an alarm?

When my attention was attracted to the subject, at first, I did suspect a young female servant, or a lad, might have pulled a bell from a childish propensity, availing themselves of the opportunity afforded by my father and mother's illnesses. I only suspected either of them, from being the youngest persons in the house, and was aware I did some things myself, which I should not have done in my mother's presence. It was with the greatest reluctance that the servant first mentioned the matter to me; and from necessity alone; to account for her coming into my mother's chamber; and from her manner, she evidently did not believe I should credit her statement. After I was convinced the bells did ring without being pulled, I examined the wires and cranks, and had the bells rung, but could not discover any thing amiss; and as a bell still continued to ring at intervals, my father ordered the bells to be carefully examined; as I then thought it might possibly arise from the bells (both of which could be pulled from the head of my mother's bed, which stood side-ways of the fire-place, and the wire did not pass over the fire) having been pulled more frequently and with greater violence, in consequence of her severe illness. The report made was, there is not any thing the matter, and the bells still continued to ring. My father was so much displeased at a servant's entering his room uncalled, that when I used to direct her to go to my father, she used to say, "my master will be very angry, and I don't think he rung the bell" - and when I went myself, he was much displeased, so that I was much distressed. I could not from principle ask a servant to do what I did not like to do myself. I could not bear the idea of my father ringing a bell when he was so ill, and not being attended to, and at which, of course, he would be highly displeased; when I went into his room he was much irritated; if possible I contrived some pretence for going into his room, but I entered trembling, and could not pursue the straightforward course of telling my father what had occurred.

If you had experienced what I did then, you would have a superior motive to investigate the cause than merely "to prevent discomfort to weak and superstitious minds."

The bells in my father's house were solemn knells: whereas the bells in your's appear to be merry peals, omens of joy. Still, though the difference is great, it is a violent ringing of a bell without apparent cause.

Should it occur again, will you ascertain the exact length of time a bell rings ? It appeared to me much longer than any bell could ring from one pull; and, if there was more than one pull, it must cause a difference in the sound: at least I should suppose so - and then how long a bell would vibrate from a violent pull, either by rope or wire ?

I asked my mother's nurse, if she had ever known or heard of bells ringing ? She looked very serious, and replied, she had several times known it in houses where she was nursing. I not only thought my father would be displeased, but I did not myself like to talk to her upon the subject, and it was hardly ever mentioned except when the ringing occurred. Both the nurse and servant were very cautious in what they said; but the servant said that every morning, for a long time past, she had always found two large winding sheets upon the candlestick from the rush-light, which my parents burnt in their room of a night; that she had done all she could think of to prevent it. Whether from the presence of malaria in the house, or from whatever cause, the candles, for some months, to my knowledge burnt always in this manner. I tried every means I could devise to prevent what was a constant source of inconvenience, trouble, and expense. The candle-sticks, tables, and glass-lamp in the hall, which hung in a well stair-case, so that you could pass to the rooms without carrying a light, were all covered with tallow. I requested the best candles might be sent – tried various shops, but all to no purpose – the candles would gutter down.

Whatever tricks servants may play, it is not likely they should, for any continuance, play such as would cause themselves extra trouble: I know of no motive which could cause any such to then be played. In the Ipswich Journal, a girl prone to mischief, duped her master into believing his afflicted wife was "bewitched;" she not only made a fool of her master, but, probably, it enabled her to neglect her mistress.

Another circumstance which the servant mentioned was the fires burning only on one side of the stoves, which continued for months. She was reluctant to state any thing which I could not do otherwise than observe myself. It was first noticed in the kitchen. My mother complained of the meat not being well roasted, and which I am convinced was occasioned by the impossibility of getting the fire to burn, except on one side of the grate. The meat was saddened, by it being so long at the fire, and had to be turned end for end before it could be done at all in any way. It was the same in all the fires, and I tried in vain to make the fires burn on both sides. My father was displeased, and said the fire in his room was not properly stirred or kept up. With respect to the coals, my father was not only particular in having the best – but much better coals are carried to the London market than any I have ever seen in Suffolk. Instead of having the coals shot down into the cellar, in the front of the house, as in London, my father had then shot down upon the premises; the round coals were then carted, and shot down into the coal cellar, and the dust of the coal was burned in the hothouse.

My parents were both persons of delicate constitutions and habits – both died of lingering disease; my mother did not change in the least, until the ninth day after her decease, and my father about the seventh – It was just sufficient to satisfy me that they were dead: - my sense of smelling was always very keen, my lungs weak and susceptible, and like Caspar Hauser*, I am often annoyed by what others don't observe. The house could be, and was, well ventilated; the chambers were free from ill smells; every attention was paid for the purpose, and I can no more account for the fires and candles than for the ringing of the bells. Still, as the bells were not the only thing in the house which were affected, with a view to elucidate the matter, if possible, I have stated these particulars, as far as my time and your patience will extend – the whole truth should be stated.

I believe there were what is called "other signs" – but nobody dared to tell me what I could not but observe myself, and for a long period.

When these facts were recent, I observed in the drawing-room of the late Mr. Opie, R.A. in Berners Street, the fire burning only one side. Mr. Opie had complained of not feeling well, but was painting in his study; and one day I was alone with Mrs Opie, I said to her, "I don't like to see the fire in this manner, as the fires did in my father's house, for some time before my parents died." She laughed, and instantly stirred the fire, with the view to make it burn more to my satisfaction. For some time previously to Mr. Opie's death, the fire in the drawing-room burnt well upon Mrs Opie's side of the fire place, but hardly ever upon Mr. Opie's side; which I observed, but was reluctant to believe that any thing was about to happen to him.

Both my parents were in the habit of looking at the barometer,

---

* Editor's note: A reference to the mysterious boy who appeared on the streets of Nuremberg in 1828

and likewise at thermometers; and directing me frequently to tell them the state of the glasses; and therefore I was in the habit of so doing – but during my parent's illnesses I seldom did so, except when requested by my father. I am not aware that there was any thing unusual in the state of the weather or the state of the glasses; and I think if there had been so, the apothecary, who was very intimate, and in the habit of looking himself in these glasses, would have mentioned it.

I don't know if I can procure a newspaper which contained your letter; but I should have liked to have sent one to my tenant, who took my father's house after his decease; but who did not remove into it until March following; which was the reason of my finally quitting till that time: - and to enquire if he has ever been annoyed by the ringing of the bells.

I have the honour to be, Sir,

Your very obedient servant,

———————

To Edward Moor, Esq.
Bealings, near Woodbridge

(in the envelope)

In addition to the inclosed, may be added, that my father had in the house, an air pump, microscope, &c. and had from his youth, made observations and experiments.

For some time, the bell in the attic rung at night as well as day, and so might the lower one, unheeded; the manner of the ring was so long and violent, and different, that upon reflection, I now think, after a time, no servant came to tell me.

The appearance of a piece meat roasting at one end, by a half fire, was heart-sickening, and most desolate to view.

Upon my mother's decease, my father desired me to take her trinkets, and I was much startled, when I looked at the diamonds, which appeared like the film of a boiled egg; but instantly disappeared, and resumed their brilliancy upon being rubbed with a handkerchief.

If any of your friends should be craniologists you may say I have the bump of inquisitiveness, which may induce me to search and enquire, into the cause of unusual appearances.

I admit, that the plundering in the house was a reason to induce Dr Alderson, to consider it an imposition upon me; but I am convinced, and particularly from the attic bell, it was not: besides what motive, or what end could it answer?

I hope you will cause the test, of the duration of time a bell rings, to be tried, if possible, to a second.

The dog, a remarkably fine, undaunted, blue or mouse-coloured, terrier, whose eminent qualifications had gained him admittance to the house, - when the attic bell rang after dark, discovered great emotion, was silent and riveted to the spot, and would not leave me: his aspect was so fierce and determined that the nurse was afraid he would seize and bite her, being a stranger; but the dog seemed to know, as well as I, that she could not have pulled the bell.

In the following month, I received another letter from the same lady, which I give, with the same cautionary omissions.

No.5

_____ , *SUFFOLK, April 2 1834.*

SIR,- Having been confined by a severe cold, I was not able to go into town till yesterday – and then could not procure a conveyance to

London for the inclosed letter. I am so deeply interested about the matter, that I regret not being able to converse with you upon the subject, as it is so difficult to get any person to believe it otherwise than trick. One gentleman, who had read your letter in the Ipswich Journal, I could not induce to think otherwise, until I mentioned bells ringing for months after they had been severed from the wires – when he began to think of electricity. Another, who had not heard before the circumstances, asked me if your house was situated on a wet or boggy soil?* as bells had been known to ring when affixed to the walls of such houses. I could only answer, that my father's house was built upon a dry, gravely soil; and had been built in so dry a season, that the slates had been put on without a drop of rain having fallen into the house. He said he should like to have some further conversation upon the subject at another opportunity, and to read your statement.

In the dead of two nights, during which the bell in the attic rung repeatedly with such extreme violence, I carefully searched the house, attended by two female servants and the dog, who left his master from this time, and kept close by me. The house, was built after the London manner, and afforded no places for concealment, and was detached. I found all doors and windows properly fastened; the trap-door in the ceiling of one of the attics through which you could go upon the top of the house, was bolted, as usual, and I did not explore under the roof; but I took the precaution of ordering the step-ladder to be removed; and after we had left the room, which was not in use, I locked the door myself, and took the key, and the next morning I went out upon the top of the house. I went into the cellars, to be satisfied there was nobody nor nothing in the house. I thought it was possible a cat or a bird might have got in, and then clawed the bell-wire. The servants readily did everything I directed; and as to the dog, in his early days he had established his

---

*Editor's Note: This idea appears to be fore-runner of a theory promoted in the mid-20th century by Guy Lambert of the Society for Psychical Research holding that underground water was responsible for many "ghostly" disturbances.

fame, by seizing and biting trespassers in the grounds by day time, and had such an aversion to vermin, that, for his own amusement, he would watch for, kill and bury frogs, which, from their extreme coldness, few dogs will touch. The dog performed his part of the search. The nurse remained with my mother; and the room door was left open, in case of our meeting with any thing. The bell rung in the attic repeatedly after the search; and I directed the servants to go to bed in a chamber adjoining my father's; for it was impossible to think of their going to bed in this attic chamber; and they removed my feather-bed, &c. from an attic chamber, above my mother's chamber, down into a corner of her room. No man servant slept in any of the attics; but there were two men servants' rooms adjoining to, but not in, the house upon the ground floor.

It was impossible for any thing to have escaped out of the house without knowledge of myself and the dog.

I had seen my father perform experiments with the air pump when a child. I was aware a bell would not ring in an exhausted receiver – and if I applied any thing to the side of the fire which would not burn, by the same rule the bells should not have rung, or but faintly, when pulled; and on the contrary, if, fixed air was rending the bells, the fires should have burnt with more than usual brightness: I thought then, and still am of that opinion, that by some means or other, it must have been occasioned by the air being condensed or rarefied, and yet no house could admit of more perfect ventilation, and no person be more susceptible than myself. The chimnies did not smoke.

The nurse said, "you'll find nothing," which somewhat emboldened us in the search; yet from fear we kept so close together, that it was any thing but a stragling party. The dog diligently searched and scented by my direction; but he did not scent as if he scented any thing himself. From the construction of the house, and with the dog's assistance, it was impossible to have made a more effective search. This I relate to refute the assertion, and suggestion to you, by the "Constant

Reader"* of the Ipswich Journal, whom I shall dismiss with the observation of Voltaire's, that "the English could not decide any matter without the wager," that I determined, and kept into such an absurd way of determining a matter.

If trick, there was a large bell, unhung, which would have been much more convenient for the purpose. It was always intended to be affixed outside the back part of the house, as had been the case where we formerly resided, and used to be rung by hand out of the window. Any person in the lower part of the house could have had access to this large bell, or moved it where they pleased.

There was likewise a small bell, which never had been hung, in a closet, with the air pump and its apparatus. This could have been still more conveniently carried and rung in various parts of the house, and would have been more effective as a trick.

There was but one stair-case, and no passage in the house; the front door from the road opened into the hall, and the back door into the lower hall; and all the rooms into these halls are upon broad landing-places.

Should you ever learn further particulars, or can discover any cause, I hope you will remember how much I am interested about the matter.

I have the honour to be Sir,
Your very obedient Servant.

This letter, I believe, closed the correspondence with the lady. I preferred giving it uninterruptedly; although pending it, another correspondent addressed me, as follows:

* No.2

No.6

NOTTINGHAM, March 15, 1834

SIR, - A friend having handed to me a copy of your letter, addressed to the Ipswich Journal, related some extraordinary circumstances connected with your residence, I am induced to take the liberty of enquiring whether you have heard the particulars of long and repeated bell-ringings in a house near Chesterfield ? If not, I shall be happy to furnish you with a general idea of the affair, and can direct you where to apply for a sight of a minute statement taken down as the events occurred. These events quite baffled the acutest enquirers; and as they occurred during the course of one or two years, many such had an opportunity of trying their skill, both when the bells were connected with lines, and when the wires had been cut off for months; a circumstance that made no apparent difference in their sounding disposition. The thing became so common at length, that to prevent the children in the family from feeling alarmed, they were led to suppose the bells were ill, upon these occasions. My friend who resided in the house is the reverse of superstitious; well educated, philosophic, and indefatigable in research; and I have not heard that he ever hazarded a guess as to the cause. And I examined every part of his extensive mansion with the strictest care, and could not divine the moving natural power adequate to the effect.

I shall be obliged by your saying if you have arrived at any more satisfactory conclusion; and for a reason to be afterwards explained, would also ask, if you have any knowledge of the Derbyshire family of the _____, or of a lady from Lancashire named _____.

I am Sir,
Your's very respectfully,
W. FELKIN.

To E. Moor, Esq

I replied to the following letter on the 21st. of March, and soon after received the following:-

No.7

NOTTINGHAM, March 27, 1834

DEAR SIR,—I thank you for your letter, with further particulars respecting the ringing of your bells, which are very interesting to myself and friends acquainted with the Chesterfield affair. It was Mr. Martin* to whom I had mentioned the extraordinary circumstances at C. who sent me your detail as a counterpart. Mr. Babbage was present at our conversation; and from the part he took it would be interested to know your dilemma, and to help you out of it philosophically; he, with yourself, deeming supernatural agency out of the question. The reason of my enquiring if you knew the ⸺'s was, because they are proprietors of Rose Hill, Chesterfield; though not resident at it – and if you knew ⸺, because she was governess in the family of Mr. James Ashwell, resident at Rose Hill during the bell-ringing; and it was barely possible that she might, for ought that appeared, be filling a similar situation in your family. The gossips of C. have found out that the bells began to ring on her entering the family – continued to ring at intervals during her stay – and ceased on her quitting the family. This is not strictly accordant with the fact – I believe – but your answer puts beyond doubt, that the same human agency could not have been employed in both cases.

In the Chesterfield case, all the bells in the house, rang at one time or another; but never before five in the morning; nor after eleven at night.†

---

* Of the Chancery Bar
† Editor's note - This is in accordance with the findings in modern poltergeist cases that the phenomena rarely occur when the human "focus" is asleep.

The cutting of wires made no difference; and the oscillation was like that of a pendulum; not a decreasing one. A bell was put up one Saturday evening, unattached to any wire, and rang in half an hour. The moveable shutter bells on the parlour window inside the shutters, when rooms were locked, and no person within such rooms, rang. A bell taken down, and laid aside in a closet, rang as it lay*.

The house is so substantial that the highest winds could not be felt: its foundations are very large; and the walls both outer and inner of stone cased with brick; of great thickness and quite solid. The bells are hung quite out of reach; and no examination resulted in detecting the least tampering with them. I heard of one very laughable incident. The bellhanger was engaged in re-attaching the wires, after a long silence, when one of the bells began to ring in his face. Upon this he dropped down the ladder, and without waiting to gather up his tools, &c. ran as fast as his legs would carry him; crying, that Satan was in the bells, and he would have no more to do with them.

As the matter remains enveloped in the same mystery, and the particulars have been carefully and fully noted down when they occurred by Mr. J. Ashwell, I shall refer you to him at 196 and 197, near Queenhithe upper Thames-street; and in his absence, if you enquire there for his private residence, in either case he or Mrs A. would, I am sure, let you hear the whole detail with great pleasure.

I can form no idea of any general law of nature that would, in its operation, produced apparently contradictory, independent, and arbitrary results, as this chain of circumstances: no human agency has appeared. It seems unlikely that any satisfactory explanation will be given of either case; although as to Chesterfield, the work-people are soon to repair, and make Rose-hill House into two residences, when perhaps, some cause may be brought to light to clear the mystery.

---

* This is believed to be erroneous.- E.M

I am, Sir,
Your's very respectfully,
W.FELKIN

To Edward Moor, Esq

At the period to which we have now arrived – toward the end of March 1834 – I was in London. And in consequence of the preceding letters, No.6 and 7, I placed myself in communication with Mr Ashwell, the gentleman therein mentioned. He favoured me with several interviews; and with the relation of many particulars of his similar visitations; and with the following note:

No.8.

UPPER THAMES-STREET, May 3, 1834.

DEAR SIR, – The paper you so obligingly sent, is at my residence at Stowell; but I will have the statement inserted by yourself copied, and return it addressed (as your note just received) on Monday.

Before the end of this week (the time of your departure) I will endeavour to write such differences as are most important, between the occurrences in our respective houses; and when I permit, I shall not omit to commit to writing a circumstantial detail of the whole – which it will give me pleasure to send you. My partner has for several weeks past been absent at our works in Scotland, which must be my excuse for not doing as I named, when you favoured me with a call.

I am, dear Sir,
Your's faithfully
JAMES ASHWELL.

Having been thus led to hope for a circumstantial account of the Derbyshire ringings from such authority, I made no notes of Mr. Ashwell's interesting communications to me. They, of course, generally accorded with those of his friend, Mr Felkin; but extended to many other particulars.

When I assented to the suggestion of printing the statement in the reader's hand, I had reason to hope that in addition to what precedes, I might be able to give also, a minute detail of the more extraordinary circumstances, just alluded to. But on applying to the gentleman in whose house, and under whose eye, they occurred, I suffered the disappointment of learning that I could not be furnished with the details; for the reason stated in the following note, which I give here, though not chronologically in its place; it being a continuation, and leading to the conclusion, of the mysterious ringings in Derbyshire:-

No.9

BLAENFOU, SOUTH WALES,
March 1, 1841

DEAR SIR, I should have had much pleasure in supplying the statement you request, and especially in aid of an object so laudable and interesting; but as a consequence of their relation to a literary friend (some time since) I am under an engagement to supply the facts for publication. You will perceive (however unwillingly) that I am thereby precluded from the gratification of your wishes. I shall feel; interested in your pamphlet; and if you will address the copy that you obligingly intend for me to the Parthenon Club, St James's Square, I shall thankfully receive it.

My engagement here has been so onerous a character, that I have been unable to do any thing towards the statement, I am pledged to produce. But I am about to remove; when my leisure will ere long, I trust, enable me to complete it. I shall have pleasure in remitting you a copy.
     I remain, dear Sir,
       Your's faithfully
        JAMES ASHWELL.

Edward Moor, Esq.

P.S. Your note, dated I see, the 16th of last month, has been delayed, from its address, to my former business connection.

Much regretting that I cannot here give, the expected relation of the very strange doings at, or near Chesterfield, from such authentic source, I will tax my recollection for some particulars, obligingly communicated to me, by Mr Ashwell, in 1834.

The house was large, and old; and, with some had the reputation of being "haunted". I forget the date of the occurrences; but believe ten or twelve years ago - say 1830 - his ringings, from first to last, continued, about eighteen months. They differed from mine, among others, in this particular: - that instead of ringing in peals (of four or five) by sudden starts and instant quietude, his rang continually; many seconds, with violent oscillations and clatter. Insomuch, that while one was in such violent vibration, he would seize it between his hands, and compel cessation. But, on being liberated, it would resume its vibration and ringing. This operation was several times performed with uniform results. His servants were much alarmed; and some left their places.* A public foot-path passed near his front door. Many passengers made a circuit rather than pass close to it.

The strange events within, were much talked of in the neighbourhood: and reasons existed to render it desirable that the matter should be less discussed and notorious.

I forget the number of bells in the house; and how many rang; whether all, or not; and if not what description most distinguished themselves, by frequency and singularity. Mr. Ashwell is a literary and scientific gentleman; and tried various experiments with electrometers and other tests: but could discern nothing, especially present or absent, giving any clue to the discovery of the cause of the strange effects witnesses. To that day – and I dare say to this – he was, and is, altogether at a loss, as to such cause.

He took the wires off. The bells continued their ringings. He took one down and laid it on a shelf in a closet. [This is believed to refer to the incident incorrectly given in page 52.] It remained there quiescent some weeks. He then took and placed or stuck, it between a wooden hat-peg batten, or spline, and the wall on which the batten was nailed: the bell began to ring immediately.

It is generally known that house, or chamber, bells, are fixed on a flexible, bent piece of iron, about a foot long. It was the end of such iron, it may be assumed, that was stuck between the batten and the wall.

My kind informant transposed his bells. And hence arose a sequence, that, however unaccountable, may be of moment, in approximations to the cause of these phenomena, if such shall ever be made. He observed that, in the course of renewals of ringing, a

*I may here note, that my servants were also frightened. One, the cook asked leave to go home – a few miles off. On returning, she said that she was more comfortable; for fearing what she saw and heard, portended ill to her, she was desirous of ascertaining the condition of a near and dear relative; who, instead of being, as she feared, worse, was she found, fast recovering from a dangerous illness.

particular bell took the lead. The bell he called No.1 - and three others, which he found usually to follow in regular succession, he called 2,3.4. If we suppose the bells to ring in this order of position - 3,2,1,4 - that is, 1 is to be the leader - 2 the second, and so on - he transposed them to let us say - this order - 4,1,3,2. No.1. still took the lead - No.2 followed - then 3 and 4: - and so on No.1. wherever placed, still leading; and the others numerally succeeding - 4 always the last.

Although I have noted four as having been so transposed, I am not confident of that having really been the number. It may have been four, or more. I am pretty sure there were four. And here something of a law, may be observed - or a constant: - and if so, a fancied, or hoped for, clue, may be faintly discerned, for the discovery of the theory of these hitherto, accountable phenomena. For that they are preternatural, it appears to me to be the wantonness of scepticism to doubt.

If I err not, my Derbyshire friend had opportunities of exhibiting his - what he, I believe also deem - preternaturalities, to men of science who were equally baffled. He, as well as I, have discoursed men of science thereon, without any explanatory results.

The question ever recurs - what can the cause be? An adequate cause must exist; for these effects, and for every effect; moral and physical, in nature. But, in this case, no one has yet pretended, as I know, to develop it.

It may be no advance to say - that, possibly, some hitherto undiscovered law of electricity or galvanism - latent - brought into activity, only by certain combinations of metallic alloys, in certain co-extension of parallelisms, straightness, or angles - certain concurring, or varied, degrees of tension - in connexion with certain conditions of atmosphere influences - acted upon by agencies, subtle and occult, &c. &c.

These possibilities - who combined eventualities may, or may not, ever be developed - may be only another link in amazing chain of results, that recent researches into the mysterious operation of electrics and galvanics, have brought under the wondering eye and contemplation of chymical philosophy.

Who can say, or imagine, where they are to end?

All this may, perhaps, be deemed the substitution of unmeaning words for unknown things: *ignotum per ignotius*. I shall blame no one who may think so, in reference to the preceding paragraph. Still, who can say that such things are impossible ? What is ?

Looking back, a few years, who could have fore-cast such imaginable things as we witness, in the every day results of certain intermixtures and tact of a few metallic plates and acidulous current ? The wonders of electro-galvanic results ? If such stupendous latent powers can be called into activity by such easy process, and still be unknown laws, who can say that another step may not lead us to the knowledge – if not of the why, to the how – to produce the feeble effects described in this little book ? - compared with which, the visible effect of an unknown cause, of electro-galvanic power, is indeed "Ossa to a wart." *

I here, unwillingly, take leave of the doings in Derbyshire: - and return to London, and May 1834.

Hearing, I forget how, of mysterious ringings in a house, No.9, Earl-street, Westminster, I made enquiry there: and found the family had moved to Islington. Thither I accordingly went: and found the lady at home.

I explained my errand, apologetically; and, by way of winning confidence, gave the outline of my story. I found that it was listened to with intense curiosity and anxiety. And the lady, in return, details her's; and in so exceedingly good a style, as to call from me the urgent request that she would obligingly commit it to writing for me – exactly, as far as she could, as she had verbally related it. To this she was so kind as to consent

While thus in conversation, her husband came in; and the subject

---

* Editor's note: The allusion is to Mount Ossa in Greece

was farther discussed. It was evidently very interesting to them both. I repeated my tale; and he re-told his lady's, with no material deviation.

The following is the communication of the Lady:

No.10.

19, ST PAUL'S TERRACE, BALL'S POND, ISLINGTON, May 17, 1834

SIR, I consider it necessary to offer some apology for not having complied with your request sooner. The truth is, Mr. Milnes has been so pressed with business that it slipped his memory; and rather than you should be disappointed, I have taken the task upon myself. But, Sir, I found it much easier to tell you of our mysterious bell-ring, than I now find it, to sit down for the purpose of giving you a written narrative of it. The fact was so simple in itself, that I hardly know how to reduce it to the form of history. However, it happened as follows: -

In the early part of February 1825, returning home from a walk (to our then residence, No.9 Earl-street, Westminster) about half-past four in the afternoon, I was astonished to find the family much disturbed at the ringing of bells in the house, without any visible cause. The first bell that rang was one in the nursery, the pull of which was at the bottom of the house, quite unconnected with any others. The bell rang several times before the rest began. Then the dining-room; next the drawing room; and so on, through the house, sometimes altogether, as if they were trying to entice each other in uproar; at others, one at a time: but always, very violently. By this time I was much alarmed, and sent for Mr. Milnes, from the wharf: who thinking to find out what ailed them, had the cases taken down, that concealed the wires. Finding this to be of no use, he next placed a person with a light in each room; while he himself held a candle under the row of bells below; but could not ascertain the slightest reason for this strange ringing, which lasted two hours and a half: nor have we ever since been able to discover more of it than we did then.

I do not know that I need mention the equally surprising effect it had on one of our servant girls. But if you have the fact, you can exercise your judgment upon it. She, from the first, was more terrified than any one else in the house; and at the last peal, fell into strong convulsions; so strong, as to require five men to hold her down. These convulsions continued sixteen hours, and were succeeded by insensibility, and a stupor, that lasted nearly a week. Every means were used to restore her: even violence was resorted to, but without effect. It is singular, that the moment she was seized with convulsive fits, the bell ceased to ring.

I shall be gratified to hear that you receive this in time.
Believe me, Sir,
Your's respectfully,
M.MILNES.

Mr. Milnes begs his kind respects.

Edward Moor, Esq.

The foregoing, however curious and strange, is not so copious as Mrs. Milnes' relation to me. And one circumstance, still in my recollection, is altogether omitted. It is this: - the servant who was frightened into fits by the ringing, was a mulatto. Undoing her neck and head dress, to give her air, it was discovered that she had an extraordinary and copious "head of hair"–which stood "widely out from her head, in all directions." This divergence, or radiation, was described to have been very striking: and, in the mind of the Lady-relator, I could discern a connection between the divergence of the hair of her servant, the continuance of the ringing and the duration of the fits.*

Possibly my smiling, or attention in some way to that supposed connection, may have been the reason of the omission in the preceding letter. I do not recollect, whether or not, Mr M. noticed the fact. It is, in the absence of knowledge, not unworthy of relation – implying, possibly, the presence or absence of extra-electric matter.

Referring back to page 28, it will be seen that I have brought the Bealings bell-ringing up only to the 27th of February, 1834.

What follow, is a continuation of my notes, made at the time, as it appears, on the 15th Match, on the original subject. It might as well, perhaps, have been given in earlier continuation: but has been deferred till now, the better to connect it with the conclusion.

I call it ~~~~

No 11.

Saturday, 1/2 past 4 p.m.
March 15, 1834.

Now returning home I am told "the bells are ringing again" – and, going into the kitchen I learn that twenty minutes to three, "the five" rang violently. Only one servant saw this – the butler. The cook was outside. The other servants variously employed, or out; and not one

*Editor's note: Fits, seizures and collapses suffered by people present in poltergeist cases have been noted by other writers and researchers. Examples include the case of Esther Cox at Amherst, Nova Scotia in 1878 (see The Great Amherst Mystery (1888) by Walter Hubbell), a case in Indianapolis in 1962 (see The Poltergeist (1976) by William G. Roll) and in the Enfield poltergeist in 1977-8 (See This House is Haunted (1980) by Guy Lyon Playfair

within reach of the wires. A second peal "of the five" about three o' clock. Three servants were present. They sent for a neighbour – a man of sagacity – who, in about three-quarters of an hour, witnessed a third peal. A few minutes after the bell of the "best bed-room" rung, singly. This is on the right of the whole – that which formerly struck the ceiling and knocked some white-wash off. The dining room bell was observed to shake: but did not ring. At one of the peals, a child of a neighbour, about nine years old was present. She was a good deal alarmed. She had heard of the ringing, and had wanted to see it. I will note, that the day is cold in the shade – the wind being sharp, in the east. The sun is rather hot. At the former ringings, the mornings had been chiefly frosty, and the days warm, for the season. It is thought, on explanation, that at the first mentioned peal of the day, only four bells actually rung – all were agitated – but the one which afterwards sounded then singly, is thought to have been silent. Barometer 30 3', thermometer 52.

The preceding extract is taken from my notes, made at the moment. Soon after, I went to London, as has been mentioned, and I received from my son, the Rev. E.J. Moor, a continuation of the subject. The following are extracts from his letters:—

No. 12.

BEALINGS, Monday, March 24, 1834.

"As I was returning from Woodbridge, on Friday, Bealings, "told me that Mr. Silver" (then and now of Woodbridge) "had lately heard from Mr. Rose, of Ramsgate" (a surgeon, recently moved thither from Woodbridge) "who informed Mr. S. that a house, near his, Mr Rose's, has been similarly affected with our's touching bells. There appears no end to the changes on these bells – "those evening bells – those morning bells." Our's have been ringing again. Last Saturday, about twenty minutes after one, all five went off, while Gurney (then and now master of the Woodbridge National School) was in the kitchen. Cook had been talking with him on the subject, and he said he should like to hear them. Wind S.W. Thermometer 49 °

"Mallet" (a painter and glazier of Woodbridge, deceased) "saw the wires shake, as I am told, and went to hear if the bells had rung."

BEALINGS, March 29, 1834.

"Thursday last, March 27, bells rung again – four bells at twenty minutes after four – five bells at twenty minutes before five."

BEALINGS, April 14, 1834.

"Mr. Silver tells me, respecting the Ramsgate bells, that Mr. Rose writes, as follows: - "It is somewhat singular that the bells in the house we are just removing to, rang several days the week before last, to the great astonishment of all in the house. We cannot account for it. It was not confined to the day. The door night-bell rang once or twice in the morning early; and we could not find out that it was done by human aid."

(Mr. Rose's letter was dated March 4, 1834.)

"Mr. Heard informed me this morning that Mr. Swindell, of Aldborough" (schoolmaster) "told him a few weeks back, that about five years ago, the bells in his father's house rang; and Mr. S. watched them narrowly. It was soon after his father's and mother's death. Mr S. was satisfied that it was some current of air which caused it."

I resume my own relation of occurrences.

The preceding extracts are made on the 11th July, 1834; up to which time, from the 29th March, no more ringings have occurred, at Bealings.* But between those dates, I have obtained much information on the subject of unaccountable bell-ringing, in other quarters – London, Derbyshire, Cambridge, Chelmsford, &c. These I shall collect, and condense, sometime or other. Within these few days, meeting on the spot, the servant, who, in my first published letter, is stated to have seen the wires shaking, he explained to me, that, being at work near, he heard them; and going to see, he perceived the external perpendicular wire† of the dining room bell, shaking violently. He then observed and heard the other wires running horizontally to the "common aperture," rattle violently; and then went to the kitchen to see and hear what was going on there.

No. 13

ALDBOROUGH ACADEMY,
September 3, 1834

DEAR SIR, - I was duly honoured with your communication concerning the mysterious bell-ringing. Allow my numerous engagements of late to apologise for my delay in acknowledging it.

The instances of bell ringing, which excited some attention and alarm in my house, occurred about nine years ago, during the

---

* Nor since. April 1841. It hence appears, that from the first ringing, on the 2nd of February, to the last, on the 27th of March 1834, was 53 days. [Editors note – actually 54 days.]

† The wire in question was then, and is, very slack, as they all seem to be – and, of course – are easily shaken. But going out, just now, April 1831 – to try, I find that I cannot shake it by blowing as hard as I can on it. I expected I should have so shaken it easily.

melancholy illness and death of the late Mr. Sparkes. A few days before his death, his bed-room bell rang twice or thrice, rather loudly, and suddenly; and on his servants or daughter's running to enquire his pleasure, they were surprised at his answering, "he wanted nothing, he had not rung." But the most alarming occurrence was after his death. In the silence and awe of midnight, as his two old nurses were sitting by his laid-out corpse, suddenly the bell had so often rung, rung violently. The maid-servant was arouse and ran to enquire the cause. None of the three can speak of the alarm felt, without feelings of dread and wonder to the present day. On my coming up to the house, for I was then a favoured visitor to the youngest daughter, I was constrained to lay aside my love emotions a little, to array myself in philosophical penetrations, and to visit the scene of mystery and alarm. It occurred to me, to pull the bell strongly, and to hold it so part of a minute. The wire being thus strained, struck fast. I put up my finger and gave it a touch, and it rang just in the sudden violent manner it had done before.

The mystery, as well as the bell were thus set at liberty, and not alarmed us since. When I next visit Seckford-hall, I should be gratified to set my philosophical wits to task on your bells and wires, as I have not much faith in ghosts, or unnatural causes.

I beg to subscribe myself, with respect.
Dear Sir,
Your obedient servant.
JOHN SWINDELL.

To Major Moor.

Among my collections on this subject, is the following, cut out of the *Morning Chronicle* of the 8th of October, 1834:-

No.14

A STRANGE VISITOR.- Considerable sensation has been excited in Greenwich Hospital during the last few days, in consequence of the following extraordinary occurrence in the apartments of Lieutenant Rivers, in that institution. In the early part of the week, the family of Lieutenant Rivers were startled, by the sudden ringing of one of the bells in the house, without any apparent cause. In a short time afterwards, the bell in another room began to ring in a similar manner, and presently the whole of the bells were in full concert together. The same circumstance occurred at intervals during the day. The closest investigation took place, but not the slightest clue could be discovered to this extraordinary affair. The bells have continued ringing in a similar manner throughout the whole week, and to this moment the cause remains an impenetrable mystery. The alarm of the female branches of the family has been so great that they have quitted the premises. The most searching enquiry has been instituted: the servants have been questioned, and persons have been stationed in different rooms at the same time; but the bells continued to ring on without the slightest clue to the agency of their action. The wires were cut off a day or two ago by Mr. Thame, of Nelson-street, and the music then ceased; but as soon as the wires were re-fastened, the bells again began their accustomed tune. *Greenwich Gazette.*

The same visitation, I also find, in my collections, were amply detailed in the Kentish Observer, of 9th October, 1834 – extracted, as it appears, from the same authority: –

No. 15.

A STRANGE VISITOR. - Considerable sensation has been excited in Greenwich Hospital during the last few days in consequence of the following extraordinary occurrence in the apartment of Lieut. Rivers, in that institution. Considerable sensation has been excited in Greenwich Hospital during the last few days, in consequence of the following extraordinary occurrence in the apartments of Lieutenant Rivers, in that institution. In the early part of the week, the family of Lieutenant Rivers were startled, by the sudden ringing of one of the bells in the house, without any apparent cause. In a short time afterwards, the bell in another room began to ring in a similar manner, and presently the whole of the bells were in full concert together. The bells have continued ringing in a similar manner throughout the whole of the week, and to this moment the cause remains an impenetrable mystery. The alarm of the female branches of the family has been so great that they have quitted the premises. The most searching inquiry has been instituted: the servants have been questioned, and persons have been stationed in different rooms at the same time; but the bells continued to ring on without the slightest clue to the agency of their action. The wires were cut off a day or two ago by Mr. Thame, of Nelson-street, and the music then ceased; but as soon as the wires were re-fastened, the bells again began their accustomed tune. *Mr Bicknell*, the solicitor to the institution, and several other keen individuals, have visited the premises in order, if possible, to unravel the mystery; but like Tom Moore's "Evening Bells," those of Lieut, Rivers, "still rung on". Friday morning, Mr. Bate called at the house, and it was shown to him, that the front door bell, which had been tied up, did not ring; but within five minutes afterwards that too, which may be considered the Great Tom of the apartments, gave out its awful admonitions. We heard this morning that the bells have been at peace since Friday noon. [M'Kenzie, in his History of Northumberland, a work of undoubted authority, also gives the following singular account of a visitation somewhat akin to the above: "In January, 1800, an invisible and mischievous apparition, played many wonderful pranks, at a place called Lark-hall, near this place (Burrowdown). The trick, and we may venture to call it such, was conducted with such surprising address, as even to puzzle the sceptic, and to set conjecture at defiance. Lark-hall is a small farm, belonging to Mr. Wm. Walby, of Burrowdown, and was then rented by Mr. Turnbull, a butcher, in Rothbury, who kept his father and mother, two old decent people, at a farm, with a hind and his family, whose characters were more dubious. The two families were divided by a partition, formed by close beds, having a narrow dark passage between. The garrets above were kept locked by old Turnbull. At the time mentioned above, knockings and noises were heard in Turnbull's house: the plates, glasses and tea ware left the shelves and were broken; the chairs and tables danced about the room in the most fantastic manner; scissors, bottles, wooden dishes, &.c flew in all directions, and sometimes wounded the confused and terrified spectators; a poor tailor was assailed with a tin pot of full of water, yet he still had the temerity to stand to his post till a large rolling-pin descended from the laths, and hit him a blow on the shoulders. But one of the most curious tricks was played in the presence of the Rev. Mr. Lauders, lately a dissenting minister at Harbottle, and who came to administer some spiritual comfort and consolation. He had been but a short time in the house, when a Bible moved from the window, in a circular manner, into the middle of the room, and fell down at his feet ! These singular and incredible facts, with many more which we have not room to mention, are certainly true, as they were attested by a host of respectable witnesses. Twenty guineas were offered for the detection of fraud, but without success. Two professors of legerdermain, besides many intelligent gentlemen examined the premises with accuracy, but nothing was discovered that could lead to detection. Mr W.W. having a reputation for skill in the sciences, was suspected. His visits to Lark-hall were frequent, but some of the most wonderful phenomena took place when he was certainly absent. Some suspicious circumstances were, however, discovered. Nothing was injured in the garret; the hind's bottles and earthenware were respected; a small iron rod was found in the passage, which fitted a hole made in the back of his bed, and the ghost left the premises shortly after the communication between the families had been nailed up. The affair still continues the subject of wonder to the credulous in almost all parts of the country. The hind's daughter, who acted a very conspicuous part in this wonderful deception, exhibits the most uncontrollable rage when any attempt is made to bring the subject forward in discourse"] – *Greenwich Gazette.*

About this time – or somewhat earlier – perhaps, I received the following anonymous note – without date – bearing the Colchester postmark: –

No.16

SIR, – Understanding that you have lately been favoured with periodical concerts from you bells; and that it has consequently occasioned no small amusement amongst your neighbours, &.c I cannot help recommending you, as I have a great respect for your name and character, to silence their tongues as well as your noisy inmates, by the speedy application of tow and twine. And with my knowledge of human nature, I venture to say, the witch will soon cease her diabolical agency, and the circumstance, at least, be a quiet wonder.

Edward Moor, Esq.

I thus give, without selection, all that I have received, or that have come to my knowledge, on the subject of my little book - regardless of the frivolity of some, and of the superstitious tendency of others. — Nor do I always attend scrupulously to chronological arrangement.

The following extract turned up accidentally this day - 10th April 1841 - among some miscellaneous memoranda. It is from "The Doctor" - Vol. 1. p.292 - implying some preternatural ringing of "Great Tom" of Oxford - which is described, with more quaintness than intelligibility, in a letter said to have been written two hours after the event - on the 13th of March, 1806: -

No.17.

"An odd thing happened to-day, about ½ past 4. Tom suddenly went mad. He began striking as fast as he could about twenty times. Every body went out, doubting whether there was an earth-quake, whether the dean was dead, or the college on fire. However, nothing was the matter; but that Tom was taken ill in his bowels. In other words, something had happened to the works: but it was not of any serious consequence, for he has struck six as well as ever; and bids fair to toll 101 times to night as well as he did before the attack."

I am not, however, so assured as the writer, that those ringings of Great Tom, did arise from derangement in the machinery of the bell.

However interesting the events described, in the preceding pages, to have happened at Bealings, were at the time of their occurrence; and for some time after; they had, of course, in the lapse of years become less so. And, although by no means forgotten, or disregarded, several years, perhaps, had passed, since I had perused, or referred to the documents in my possession on the subject.

Recently, however, for, and in, the cause before described, the whole of my materials came under critical review, and consideration. And I have found no reason to alter my earlier conceptions on the mysterious affair.

Re-perusing, and re-considering the papers – Nos. 14, 15, page 66 – containing the relation of the event at Greenwich Hospital, similar to that at Bealings; it occurred to me, that – as in the case of my first published account, in the Ipswich Journal – No.1. preceding – the publication in the Greenwich Gazette, led, probably to communications to, or comments by, the Editors of that or other Journals. And it further occurred to me, that I had an old friend and fellow soldier, then, and now residing at Greenwich: and that it was likely that he was informed of the transaction at the time; and might have it in his power to communicate something possessing interest; or to point out how I might obtain such information, by enquiries in other quarters.

My old friend – of more than half a century – Colonel Forman – of the Bombay army – now, and for many years, a very active magistrate of the county of Kent – has accordingly, favoured me with sundry papers, connected with the mysterious ringings in Greenwich Hospital.

My little book was in type up to the 70th page, when I made the application to my respected friend. And I received, very opportunely, the communications that I am now about to introduce, in continuation, on the 4th of May, 1841.

The most important is from Lieut. Rivers himself – in whose apartments in Greenwich Hospital, the ringings occurred: addressed to Col. Forman. It is, in the main, similar to what has been already given from the Greenwich Gazette of 3rd October, 1834 – No.14, page 66, and No.15 page 67. But as it contains several other curious particulars, it is highly deserving of entire insertion.

I call it No.18

No. 18

The bells in my apartments in Greenwich Hospital, from some unknown cause, commenced ringing at half-past six o'clock, on the morning of the 20th September, 1834; and continued, first one, and then another, at intervals of five or ten minutes, and sometimes all four at once. The first day, I had a minute examination, made by the clerk of the works, and the bell-hanger; and in the evening, at eight o'clock, I had the wires cut off from them. The bells, then ceased to ring; but the wires, were agitated, for some minutes afterwards. All remained quiet, during the night. At nine o'clock next morning, the bell-hanger came, and re-united the wires to the bells; which had no sooner been done to the first, when it rang; the second the same; and they continued at intervals, as before all that day; and many persons witnessed the performance. In the evening, about eight o'clock, I tied up the clappers; while so doing, the bells were much agitated and shook violently. They ceased to ring, during that night. In the morning I loosed them again; when they began to ring again. The clerk of the works, his assistant, and Mr Thame, the bell-hanger, came; and had another examination, without discovery as to the cause. They requested the family and servants would leave the apartments to themselves. We did so; and dined at four o'clock, at our neighbour's opposite; and while at our dinner there, we heard the bells ring a peal. Mr. Thame and the assistant to the clerk of the works, remained until eleven at night; one watched the cranks, the other the bells below, with perfect astonishment: but they ceased at their accustomed time, about nine o'clock or half-past. At eleven o'clock I requested them to retire, having made up my mind to sleep there by myself: but my brother-in-law, Capt. Watts, and my wife, determined likewise to do so. I searched the apartments, before I went to bed: and retired at half-past eleven o'clock. In the morning, they began to ring again; but more faintly than before. I was then fully resolved, to let them have their play out. Several scientific men, tried to discover the cause. The fore door bell was detached from the others, which did not ring. I secured the door pull, to prevent its being used: leaving the bell to have full play. On the Friday, about three o'clock in the afternoon, I went home; and found many persons, satisfying their curiosity; and when explaining to them, that I thought it very extraordinary, that the fore door bell did not join with the others in the performance, it immediately set up a good ring; and since which, we have heard no more of it; and the cause remains still mysterious. I have heard, that the same circumstances occurred, in another officer's apartments, in the hospital; and it continued for a week. But he thinking it a trick of a friend, he had in his house, took but little notice of it; although his servant felt much alarmed. I must here mention, that what appeared most extraordinary, was the movement of the cranks: which the bell-hanger said, could not cause the bells to ring without being pulled downwards; which they did of themselves, in every room; working like pump-handles, Now, Sir, if your friend, has ingenuity enough, to discover the cause, I should much wish to know it. I send you herewith, a part of the Greenwich Gazette, by which you will see the statement pretty correct.

[The accompaniment referred to in the last paragraph is the same as that already given in p.67. No.15 with, however, to me, a new incident – of which further mention will be found in p.75.]

Annexed to the above communication is the following: -

No. 19

A gentleman, whom I do not know, called on me, and stated that his father took a house in the country, that had been a lady's school. The dinner bell rang frequently during the night; and the bells in the house, were frequently ringing. He tried an experiment, by fixing a bell to the wall; and it rang and upon one occasion, the piano in the parlour played, without any visible cause.

The following is also annexed to Lieut. Rivers' communication: -

No.20.

In Bell's Weekly Messenger, for 23rd January, 1841, a case is stated that the church bells of Prestbury played the chimes for 3 hours; and when they ceased, the clock struck 300 times.

And the following slip, cut from Bell's Weekly Messenger, of 23rd January, 1841 - above-mentioned - formed an enclosure in the packet of my kind friend, Co. Forman. It is taken from the Cheltenham Chronicle: -

No. 21.

A few days ago, the following curious circumstance occurred in the peaceable little village of Prestbury\; - the village chimes commenced playing at the usual time, and, to play for three hours before they stopped. No sooner had they ceased to vibrate than the clock began to strike, and struck 300 before the physical force of the whole village could stop it. This curious clock seems to have solved the perplexing problem which has puzzled all animated philosophers - perpetual motion. - *Cheltenham Chronicle.*

Prestbury is a very pretty village, within a pleasant walk of a mile, eastward from Cheltenham.

"The accompaniment," noticed in the brackets after No.18 in page 73 was a cut, as mentioned out of the Greenwich Gazette of 3rd October, 1834 - already given, No.15 - but containing "to me a new incident" - touching which reference is made to this page. It is this: -

No.22

As I have no acquaintance in Sevenoaks, I took the liberty of addressing a line to the "Officiating minister" there - giving an outline of my object; and requesting his kind of assistance in the good work on hand, by communicating to me all the particulars of which he might be in possession, or could collect, referring to the mysterious and lengthened ringings at Sevenoaks.

LONDON, May 1841.

Being in London, I sought an introduction to Lieut. And Mrs Rivers, at Greenwich Hospital. I first saw the lady, and she obligingly related the occurrences that had caused so much surprise in her house; and listened, with interest, to my relation of the similar occurrences in mine. When Lieut. Rivers came in, we had repetition of our stories. The lady related the events so well, that I was, as on a former similar occasion (see p.59) induced to take the liberty of asking her to commit them to writing. To this she obligingly assented - and the communication that will presently be given - No.23 - is the result.

Lieut. Rivers conducted me over his apartments; and minutely explained every particular. Another gentleman was, accidentally, present, who witnessed the transaction with amazement at the time - and was also communicative. I may notice that Lieut. Rivers has been a comrade of Nelson's - has lost a leg in the service. He and his lady are very intelligent and seemed the reverse of superstitious. Neither of the parties had any suspicion of a trick having been played on them - To this day, as in that, the affair, is altogether inexplicable.

No.23

GREENWICH HOSPITAL,
June 1, 1841.

The commencement of the ringing of the bells in the apartment of Mr. Rivers, Greenwich Hospital, was from Tuesday until Friday, in October 1834. As we sat at breakfast in the dining-room, the servant, not attending in the room, came in to ask, if I wanted any thing in my room; for the bell had rung twice, which she had answered each time, and found no one there. I said I had not been there, and did not want her; and thought no more of the occurrence. At half-past nine, I went into the park, as usual, for my morning walk, where I remained two hours: and on my return home found both the servants at the door, looking quite terrified. On making inquiry what it all meant, they said, they had been unable to attend to any thing for the bells, which had not ceased ringing ever since I went out. I thought it strange; but said it must be mice or wires entangled. I had been in but a short time, when the bells begun again. I was astonished, and could not account for it. They rang with great violence; first one and then another, and then all together. The bell ropes, as if in a gale of wind, swinging about and no one near them. Sometimes the cranks would turn quite straight up, and return again without making the bell sound. Means were resorted to, to find the cause, without effect; and at night we had the bells cut from the wires. The wires then continued to be much agitated, as if some one was pulling them with great violence. The next morning, the bell-hanger came to repair them: and to our surprise each bell as it was hung, began to ring. The poor man appeared much frightened, and declared he had never seen the like before. Mr Rivers then tried to tie the clappers to prevent their ringing, but could not succeed: they shook with violence out of his fingers. They remained in the same way for four or five days, ceasing at night. The house was thrown open during the day, that any person might see them and account for so strange and extraordinary an occurrence. The house was only left by the family for a few hours, during the last day of their ringing: when Mr. Thame, the bell-hanger to the hospital, and other officers of the works, took charge; and during that time the bells rang but little, apparently exhausted. At last Mr. Rivers, was shewing the situation of the bells to a party of persons, who came from curiosity, and to try and discover the cause; when the door bell, which had not rung before, and which had been nailed up (it being detached from the others) gave a tremendous peal; and all ceased from that time. It was supposed then by the party present, that it was a servant who was near where the wires communicated with the bell; and that she had pulled it. It did appear very likely, it being detached from the others; and she was suspected by many to have been the cause of the others ringing; and was therefore examined by several persons without betraying herself, or giving the slightest reason for us to think she was concerned in the affair. This is the best account, that Mrs. Rivers can give from recollection of the occurrence.

It appears from the preceding communication, that a party, to whom Mr. Rivers was shewing how his bells had rung, witnessed one ringing of one bell – that of the door – which had 'till that time, been quiet: - and they suspected that one of the servants had pulled it. And she was farther "suspected of having been the cause of the others ringing." That party, it may be observed, saw or heard one bell, ring once. That bell was especially pointed out to me. It is so situated, as to be easily reached by the hand of any one. And had nothing else occurred, that one "peal" - although described as "tremendous," by Mrs Rivers, would have caused little, if any surprise. But, taken as a whole, the mysterious ringings, caused no small surprise in all who witnessed them.

Taking leave of the Greenwich Hospital-ringings it may not be amiss to note, and apologise for some repetitions in the accounts given thereof - in p.71 and others, preceding - Nos. 14, 15, 18. I received these communications at different times, before this little book was prepared for the press; and during its being pirated: as is occasionally noted.

About the time to which we have now arrived - May 1841 - I received a notification from the resident minister of Sevenoaks, that he had not before heard of any which could give rise to my enquiry as noted in p.75.

But - while so pursuing the course of my enquiries into such matters, as came accidentally, as it were, to my hearing, I was informed that something - bell ringing, perhaps, and other mysteries - had taken place in the village of Sydersterne, in Norfolk.

I, again, took the liberty of addressing the Officiating minister, there - stating my object, in so doing, and asking the favour of the communication of particulars.

The answer - No.24 - I give without comment: doing here no more than returning my cordial thanks, to the reverend writer for his prompt and obliging reply. I give it, without abridgement or alteration although a passage relating to myself might be omitted.

No.24

SYDERSTERNE PARSONAGE
Near Fakenham, Norfolk,
Tuesday Evening, May 11, 1841.

SIR, You have indeed sent your letter, received yesterday to the House of Mystery. In the broad lands of England you cannot, perhaps, find such another. But I regret to add, that I can afford you no assistance in the "Bell" line. I have no doubt but your work *will* be very curious. I shall look out for its announcement in the Norwich Papers, and feel gratified to be a purchaser.

"OUR noises," in this Parsonage, are of *graver* character. Smart successions of "Tappings," - "groanings" - "cryings," - "sobbings," - "disgusting scratchings," - "heavy trampings," - and "thundering knocks," - in all the rooms and passages, - have distressed us, here, for a period of nearly "*Nine Years*," during my occupancy of this Cure. They, *still*, continue - to the annoyance of my family, the alarm of my servants, and the occasional flight of some of them. And I am enabled, clearly, to trace their existence in this Parsonage, to a period of Sixty Years past. I have little doubt either that, were not all the residents anterior to that time (in fact of a former generation) now passed away, I could be able to carry my successful scrutiny "*on, and on!*"

In 1833, and 1834 - we kept almost open house to enable respectable people who were personally known by, or introduced to, us to satisfy their curiosity. But, our kindness was abused, - our motives misrepresented, - and even our characters maligned. We, therefore, closed our doors; and they remain hermetically sealed!

In 1834 - I had prepared my "Diary" for publication. My Work was purchased by Mr. Rodd, the eminent Bookseller, of Newport Street, London, but as the "End" had *not* arrived, I postponed my intention from day to day, - and year to year, - in the hope of such consummation.

But the "Noises" occasionally recur, and my "Diary" occasionally progresses, until it has, now, assumed rather a formidable appearance.

Nothing can be more laudable than your generous, and Christian object, proposed by the sale of your work in question; and the favourable results of which will, I respectfully trust, equal your most sanguine hopes.

Suffer me, again, to express my regrets for being unable in any way to forward your object: whether from personal experience or the experience of friends. I assure you I shall hear, with pleasure, of your being more fortunate in your application to *others*.

I have the honour to be,
SIR,
Your obedient Servant,
JOHN STEWARD, Clk.

The extraordinary events – albeit not exactly of bell-ringing – related in the foregoing letter, could not but excite corresponding interest in my mind: and my early impression was to apply to my obliging correspondent for farther particulars. But seeing that a separate publication was intended, descriptive of those events, I abstained.

Pending these enquiries on my part, a very kind neighbour essentially promoted them, by writing to a lady in Gloucestershire, whose house had been mysteriously visited. My kind neighbour had, some time ago, mentioned there the subject of the extraordinary bell-ringings at Bealings. The lady, and I believe her husband, were reasonably enough, disposed to think that a trick had been played on my family. Now, I believe, they are persuaded differently. Stapleton is three miles from Bristol. The following is the reply to my kind friend's enquiry: –

I call it No.25.

No.25.

STAPLETON GROVE,
May 8, 1841.

MY DEAR MRS. SHAWE,* - Our extraordinary bell-ringing made such an impression on me, that I shall be able to give you a tolerably correct sketch of the circumstances: and being quite satisfied of the accuracy of my statement, I have not the least objection to your friend's mentioning name and place. Of course he will state it in his own language, not as my narrative.†

One afternoon in July 1836, the bell of one of the sitting-rooms was observed to ring loudly several times: no person having touched it. In the course of half an hour the same thing occurred with nearly (if not) every bell in the house. Sometimes one would ring singly; then three or four together. The wires were distinctly seen to descend, as if pulled violently. I sent for the bell-hanger; but before he arrived, the noise had ceased. He examined all the wires, without being able to discover any cause for this singular occurrence; and was about to take his leave; as it was growing dusk, when the bells again began to ring more violently than before. Once, we particularly noticed at this time, belonging to a room immediately over the passage in which the bells hang. It is pulled by drawing up a little slide against the wall; and the wire merely passes through the floor of the bell below. This slide we watched for more than five minutes. It was constantly shaken; even making a rattling noise, and the bell ringing. When it had continued about an hour, I desired the bell-hanger to take down every bell; as our only chance of passing a quiet night. The maid-servants (who, as you may imagine, were a good deal alarmed) assured me that the wires continued to shake through the

* Of Kesgrave Hall, near Woodbridge.
† As I cannot improve on the language, I prefer giving the narrative as I find it. I trust I commit no impropriety in so doing.

night: but I cannot vouch for the correctness of this statement, and think it was probably a little fancy on their parts. The weather was rather hot; but we were not aware of any thunder during that week. I think it impossible that there could have been any trick, as I assembled all the servants in one place, and had the house thoroughly searched. The bells had all been newly hung about twelve months before, with stout copper wire. They were all replaced the next morning, and have never shewn a disposition to be riotous from that time. I trust I have been sufficiently explicit for your friend's purpose; and we shall be very glad to read his report of similar occurrences, and the manner in which he accounts for them. We have always supposed it to have been caused by electricity.

Mr Castle* joins me in kind remembrances, and believe me, your's truly,

MARY CASTLE.

At this time – June 1841 – a kind friend in Norfolk, sent me the following – cut out of a recent newspaper. I give it a place, as I have some other mysterious doings, albeit not exactly of the description of "Bell-ringing": - and I give it without comment: - farther than remarking that "Haunted House" stories, from the time of the Cock-Lane tricks[†], to this, have been detected as impostures, or otherwise accounted for: but Bell-ringings have not, as far as I know. These mysteries of Windsor, may, perhaps, be explained, before my little book appears.

* Michel Hinton Castle, Esq

[†] Editor's note: A reference to the infamous story of the knocking ghost which allegedly infested a house in Cock Lane, London in 1762 which were ascribed to tricks played by a servant girl rapping on a wooden board.

No.26

A HAUNTED HOUSE

WINDSOR – Tuesday*

For some few days past Windsor and its immediate neighbourhood, have been in a state of considerable excitement, in consequence of a house known as "Want's-cottage," standing alone, surrounded by its grounds, at Clewer, about a mile from the town having been reported, from the extraordinary noises which have been heard there, to be "haunted". The house is occupied by Mr and Mrs. Wright (who have for some years past retired from business) their two daughters, and a female domestic. The noises which have been heard, and which are continued in intervals throughout the night and day, resemble those which would be caused by a person rapidly striking his knuckles against the panel of a door, for two or three seconds. In order to attempt to unravel the mystery, several magistrates of the county, clergymen, and the most influential residents in the neighbourhood, have visited the house, the whole of whom have been present during the time the extraordinary noises have been repeated; and, although they have evidently proceeded from a door leading from the kitchen into the water-closet in the house, close to which the parties have stationed themselves, they have been unable to throw the least light upon the affair. The following magistrates of the county, and other gentlemen residing within a short distance of the house, were present during a part of yesterday and Saturday: Mr. W.F. Riley, Forest-hill; Mr. W.B. Harcourt, St Leonard's-hill; Major General Clement Hill; Mr. Edmund Foster,

*Tuesday the 8th of June, 1841 – it is believed. Or it may be 15th June.

Clewer house; the Rev. Mr.Gould, Clewer, &c. The sound clearly proceeds from the door I have described, and can only be in any way imitated, and upon that door only, by striking the knuckles hard and rapidly upon the centre of the panel. Mr. Riley and Lord Clement Hill stationed themselves in the hall, within three yards of this door; and, as soon as the knocking commenced, rushed to the spot within a second afterwards, but not a soul was near it, and the whole of the family were in a different part of the house. The knocking is so loud that it is heard by the inmates of the houses, 400 or 500 yards off. Such is the alarm these strange, and at present unaccountable, noises have caused throughout the neighbourhood, that a lady named Roberts, who resides some distance from Mr. Wright, and whose house is divided from his two public roads, has given notice to her landlord that she will quit today; and Mr. Wright's family are represented to be in that state of mind, that they are making preparations to leave the house immediately. The whole of the machinery of the water-closet has been removed, the flooring taken up, and the ground excavated, under the impression that the nose might have proceeded from air in the pipes or drains, or from some other cause connected with this part of the interior of the house; but the noise still continues, as before at intervals: and to-day and yesterday it was even more violent and loud than ever. In order to ascertain if the door of the closet was stuck, a small piece of chip was laid upon the projecting portion of the panel, and after the knocking had ceased, this had fallen on the floor; and on Sunday last, still more clearly to ascertain this fact, Mr. Wright's son, who had arrived that morning from Newbury, fastened up the door by means of a piece of wire; and, after the noise had ceased, the wire upon examination, was found broken, and the door forced inwards. At one time the door was broken off its hinges, and placed at the back of the closet, but the knocking was precisely the same as before. The landlady of the house (Mrs. Stokes) has arrived from town, and has since caused every inquiry to be instituted, but without the least hopes at present of unravelling the extraordinary mystery. It should be observed that at three or four times when the knocking took place, there were five persons, and sometimes more, present from Windsor and elsewhere, who were determined, if possible, to detect the cause; and who were totally unconnected with family residing in the house: but they were still left in ignorance of its origin, and without the means of accounting for it. On Saturday last, a gentleman volunteered to sit up with Mr. Wright during the whole of that night. This offer, at the suggestion of the magistrates, was accepted. The rest of the family retired to rest at the usual hour, and up to six o'clock the next morning, no noises were heard; but in the course of Sunday they were more violent than ever. Many ignorant persons, of course, ascribe the noises to some supernatural agency: and a tale is now current, that some person left that neighbourhood some time back in "a very mysterious manner," and that, "no doubt a murder was committed near the spot". However this may be, gentlemen of high standing in the county (magistrates, clergymen, and others) have visited the house during the past week; and certainly, to say the least, they are all exceedingly puzzled at the extraordinary noises they have heard, within three or four yards of the spot where had stationed themselves. This singular affair continues to excite the most intense interest, and to be wrapped in the greatest mystery.

Another copy was sent to me, after the preceding in the printer's hands; cut from the *Morning Post*, of 18th June, 1841. It was obligingly forwarded to me from Lieut. Rivers, of Greenwich Hospital. It is transferred to that paper from the Standard.

Encouraged by the result of my application to the Officiating Minister at Sydersterne, as giving in No.24. p79 I similarly addressed the Officiating Minister at Prestbury - pointed to in Nos.20, 21. and learned, in reply, that no foundation, as far as he had heard, existed, for the reported mysterious chimings and ringings at that quiet village.

He obligingly directed my attention to certain "ringings" at Stapleton, "as probably well worth my enquiries:" the account of which was already in my possession - as given in p.81. No.25.

It must, on reflection, seem strange that no foundation should have existed, on which to build the story referring to Prestbury. Falsehood embellishes and magnifies; but is not often found to be altogether creative.

In page 64 it is mentioned that I had heard of unaccountable bell-ringings at Cambridge, Chelmsford, &c - and, "that I intended, sometime or other, to collect and condense such information as I could, thereon." The time has arrived - and in carrying into effect my said intention, I made enquiries at Cambridge. I learned that such occurrences had taken place there - years ago. To what extent, I did not proceed to enquire: for I was told that the family wherein they had happened, had reasons for wishing that publicity should not be given, to what was rumoured to have occurred. I sought no farther.

And in reference to Chelmsford, having no acquaintance there, I, as in some other similar cases, took the liberty of addressing, enquiringly, the Officiating Minister of that Town. Awaiting his reply, I learned that the events, the object of my questionings, had taken place in the house of Mr. Haycock, a professional gentleman of that town - and that they were of a very mysterious and surprising description. In consequence, I made free to write to Mr. Haycock; requesting as many particulars as he could recall to his recollection – of date, continuance, &c. &c. The following is the result.

I call it No.27. –

No.27.

CHELMSFORD,
6th-28mo – 1841.

George Haycock's respects to Major Moor, and in reply to his note received yesterday, informs him, that the unaccountable bell-ringing, some years since that occurred in his house, still remains a mystery. It occurred frequently – and always of an evening – for some weeks duration, and much to his annoyance. Two superior bell-hangers, on the watch, when on the steps, or ladder, holding the wires, could both see and feel the wire in action through their fingers.

The writer's numerous engagements in business prevent further communication at present.

In page 83, I have hinted that the recent "mysteries of Windsor," as given in No.26 – "may probably be explained, before my little book shall appear." By the following relation, they have been in part "explained" – by a supposed detection of imposture. It is taken from the Standard of 26th June, 1841. The matter of No.26 was printed off before that date.

No.28.

THE "HAUNTED" HOUSE AT CLEWER, NEAR WINDSOR.

The extraordinary knocking (supposed to be against the door of the water closet) having still continued with even increased violence, an intelligent man, belonging to the Windsor police, has been stationed on the premises during the past week : and, notwithstanding he has frequently been within two or three yards of the spot whence the sound preceded, at the very time, he has not been able to make the least discovery of its apparently mysterious origin.

A scientific gentleman, from London, having seen in the papers an account of the noises heard in the house, has visited the premises three times during the last ten days (the last time was on Monday, at the request of the tenant) and tried various experiments to endeavour to discover the cause, but without the least success. The boards of the floor, both inside and around the closet, have been taken up, and excavations made to the depth of several feet. The drain has been opened and closely examined, and the party has even gone so far with his experiments as to have the water in an adjoining ditch analysed ! Mr Manly, the parish sexton, attended with the grave grave-digger's sounding iron, and sounded the ground, within and without, to the depth of upwards of five feet, but no clue was obtained and the knocking still continued at intervals as before. On Monday last the noises were more frequent and violent than ever. The policeman, who was on the alert during the whole day, counted, within twelve hours, thirteen distinct knockings of the same character as have been before described.

On the following day (Tuesday) at twelve o' clock, the family removed from the house, taking with them the whole of their furniture. Previously to their leaving the knocking came on, at half-past seven o' clock that morning, the policeman being there.

As an extraordinary sensation was created throughout the neighbourhood on the subject, as well as certain suspicions excited, four respectable gentleman of Windsor, were determined to ascertain if the noise had been caused by means of trickery (which was strongly suspected) or not. They, therefore, by permission of the agent of the party to whom the property belongs, agreed to go the house that evening, and remain there during the whole of the night. They did so, accompanied by the policeman and two other persons who resided in the neighbourhood. From nine o' clock (the hour at which they arrived) until eight o'clock the following morning (when they left) not a sound was heard, nor did either the candles or the fire burn blue. The policeman has been in the house ever since, and not the slightest noise has been heard.

It does certainly appear exceedingly strange, that these "mysterious," and by some called "supernatural noises" should have ceased from the time of the family leaving the house. If it were a trick, of which there can now be little doubt, it was an exceedingly clever, although a very mischievous and wanton one. It appears to be a second edition of the Cock-lane ghost.

Agreeing with the Editorial remark in the last paragraph – that "if it were a trick, of which there can now be little doubt, it was exceedingly clever, although a very mischievous and wanton one" – I will venture the remark, that the proof, as to trick, is by no means clear. The close watching of the four respectable gentlemen, and the cessation of the sound, appear to have been coincident. Still – that they were cause and effect, is not proved: though very liable to suspicion. The sound might then have ceased, had there been no watching. As in the Bealings case: - suppose – that on the 53rd* - the last –day of our ringings, as noticed on page 64 I had got four respectable gentlemen to watch with me – and then bells had then ceased; it would no doubt, have been a strong evidence of a trick – but no proof.

---

* Editor's note: Actually the 54th day

In the course of these enquiries, I heard of a house in ~~~~~~shire having had "mysterious visitations;" - occupied by a clergyman, and his lady well known to me. I caused application to be made - that I might be favoured with the particulars. And I received the following communication - written, or about 28th June, 1841.

The writer has reasons for not giving his name, or locality; and, I have omitted all names. I therefore note that he is a gentleman of unimpeachable veracity - and of deservedly high estimation.

No.29.

THE _____ HOUSE GHOST

The facts I am about to tell, belong to _____ House - or _____ as it was formerly called; _____ a respectable old manor house in the north-eastern part of _____ shire. It was, in very early times, the seat of the _____; a family of some distinction in the County. In about the year 1680, the chief part of the ancient manor seems to have been pulled down, and the present house erected in its place; the remaining portion of the old house, being allowed to stand; and separated only by a party wall, became thenceforth a farm-house; occupied by the tenant of the adjoining lands.

The estate came into possession if the present owner's father in the year 1818; at which time the house had the reputation of being "haunted;" and many tales were told among neighbouring villagers, of uncouth sights and sounds. From which it gained that ill-repute. It was not until 1823 that Mr _____ 's family resided constantly at _____. During their occasional visits there, the peculiar noises of which I am about to speak, were often heard: but from the circumstances above related of the old house, which joined the back part of the mansion, being occupied by a farm establishment, they were thought nothing of; being attributed by the family in the mansion to their neighbours in the farm, and by the inhabitants of the farm, to their neighbours in the mansion: each party wondering exceedingly what the other could be doing at so late an hour, as that at which the sounds were heard!

About fifteen years ago the old farm-house was taken down, to be re-built at a greater distance from the mansion. During the progress of this work, a man was constantly employed in watching round the premises, to guard the timber. This man has often solemnly declared, that as he went his rounds – he saw .....! But this may have been fancy – and I believe it was: the poor man's ears having inspired his eyes with an unnatural susceptibility of vision: but what he *heard* was not to be mistaken. It was the same the family had heard for years; and have heard, almost nightly ever since. He described it, "as a great thumping noise – as if some one was beating heavy blows with a great mallet in the hall." The hall is exactly in the centre of the house, over against the spot where the old farm-house stood; and therefore very near to the place where he watched.

This is as good a description as can be given of the peculiar sound, which is known familiarly in the family as "The Ghost". In the dead of night, when every member of the family is gone to bed, and there is no imaginable cause to be assigned for them; a succession of distinct and heavy blows are heard, as of some massive instrument upon a hollow wall or floor. These sounds are seldom heard more than once in the night; and generally between the hours of twelve and two. They are sometimes so loud, as to awaken one from sleep, and startle even those who are most familiar with them. At other times almost inaudible: sometimes struck with great rapidity; at other times more slowly and leisurely: varying in duration also in about the same degree. But, whether in his noisier, or more gentle, movements, the ghost is so peculiar in his sound, as not to be easily mistaken by those who have once heard him ! No one has been able to determine from what part the sound proceeds – nor, indeed, to say with what certainty that it is within the house at all. But in whatever part you may be listening, it seems to come from some remoter corner. Thus - if you hear it, being in the drawing room, at one extremity of the house, "The Ghost" appears to come from the library at the other end: if you are in the library, it sounds as if proceeding from the drawing-room. At another time, it seems to come from underneath the stable-yard; or lawn; or in the cellar.

Considerable pains have been taken, at different times, to ascertain from whence the sounds proceed, with a hope of finding some sufficient cause of them: but entirely without success. And after about twenty years, we are entirely in the dark as ever. The length of time it has been heard, ; the fact of every domestic of the family having been often changed during the time; and the pains that have been taken to investigate the matter, while every member of the family except the watcher has been in bed - have put the possibility of any trick, out of the question: and have no less convinced the inmates that it cannot be accounted for, on any of the usual suppositions, "of horses in the stable, kicking:" or "dogs rapping with their tails;" or "rats jumping in the tanks and drains beneath the house". Horse stamp, and dogs rap, and rats gallop; but they do not make such sounds as that - one, startling, and peculiar noise, with which our ears are so familiar !

To convey a notion of the nature of "The Ghost;" and of the force, and violence, with which it sometimes bursts out, I will describe the way it has repeatedly been heard, by differing members of the family. On one occasion, it burst forth with so much violence, that the writer of this, accustomed as he was to hear and disregard it, sprung out of bed: and ran to the landing at the head of the stairs, under a conviction that the outer door of the house had been burst with violence. After a few moments, the sound ceased, and he retired to bed again: it was "The Ghost." On another occasion, when he was going up to bed, "The Ghost" began to thump violently, in the direction of the brew-house; and continued so long, that he had time to go back to the back door of the house, and sally forth in quest. On his arrival, nothing was to be heard or seen.

On another occasion, the sound having for a considerable time appeared to have come from a direction that suggested it to spring from some loose vessels in the brew -house, or from the cellar, which was close adjoining; the writer, with two of his brothers sat up: one in the cellar, and the others in the brew-house. He in the cellar did not hear it. The two who watched exactly where it had appeared to be, for a good while before, heard it, loudly and distinctly as ever: but it sounded underneath the lawn, fifty yards away from where they were !

About a month ago, the owner of the house, and a friend who happened to be staying on a visit, occupied adjoining apartments. One morning, at the breakfast table, each demanded of the other, an explanation of his movements on the previous night: each having been astonished at hearing, as he thought, his neighbour moving about and making a great noise, among his books, or the furniture of his apartment. "I expected" - said one - "to see you open my door and walk in." "I thought you must have been ill and had almost gone in to see" - said the other. Each had been quiet in bed; and the sound was nothing but "The Ghost".

The usual sound is that described; as a succession of deep thumps; but other sounds, almost more curious and unaccountable, are often heard, of which I will relate a few particulars.

Some time ago, a gentleman, a relation of the family was on a visit to _____ House. One morning at the breakfast table, he related the following curious and unaccountable circumstance: he had been awakened in the night, by hearing, as he thought, a cart, drawn along on the gravel road, immediately under his windows: it appeared to be heavy laden; and rattled, as if with a load of iron rods. Wondering what could be about at that hour of the night, he got up and opened his window, to investigate; there was neither sight nor sound of any thing to cause the noise. He got into bed again, and thought it possible he had been dreaming: but half an hour after, as he lay awake, he heard the very same again : the rattling of a loaded cart upon the drive beneath his windows. "Now" thought our friend, "I'll find the cause." So up he got again - opened his windows and looked out - but all was still. He went to bed again, and heard no more. He told the story in the morning; and enquired if any thing had taken place to cause the sound he heard. But nothing could be thought of to account for it - and he tells the story to this day.

To this, it may be well to add to other anecdotes of our nocturnal friend. Four or five years ago, the writer of this ghost history, was in the habit of sitting up at night, to a very late hour, reading in the library: and though the family are all too much familiar with our "Ghost" to be disturbed by any of his gambols; the sounds that used to strike his ears, were often most remarkable and startling. On one occasion, in particular, it seemed as if a flock of sheep from the adjoining paddock, had rushed by the windows on the gravel drive. It was not a windy night; and so convinced was he, after attentive listening, that it was the rapid rushing of a flock he heard, that he considered with himself the propriety of going out to drive them back again: but idleness prevailed : it was cold : he was busy so he voted it, "The Ghost," and sat still at his books. But when he came down in the morning, fully expecting to find marks of sheep and damage done; to his surprise, there was no sign at all of any such invasion. The lawn was smooth and the gravel was untrodden; and it was, indeed, "the Ghost!"

At another time it happened that when the whole family were in one room, at prayers - not one member absent but a young child in the nursery - a noise was heard, as of some one walking across the hall, next to the room in which they were assembled. The lady who was reading prayers, rose from her knees directly, and went into the hall with the servants at her heels, before it was possible a person could have gone away : but there was no one to be seen; nor any thing to lead the supposal of a visitor of any more substantial kind, than our old friend "The Ghost!"

It should be mentioned here, that there is, running underneath the house, a very large old drain which has been thought to be connected with the sounds above described. A few years ago - this drain was thoroughly examined, with a view to ascertaining whether some loose brick, or timber, might be lying in it, which might create such sounds, on being trod upon by rats, &c. A man was sent up through it, from one end to the other; but nothing of the kind appeared. The whole was thoroughly and carefully cleared out, but the noise proceeded on, as ever. How long "The Ghost" had been observed before the present family resided is not known : but the popular belief attaches all the unblest circumstances here related to the unquiet spirit of one Squire _____ , a man of but indifferent repute, as it would seem : and one, whose grave might not be found an easy resting place. The old Squire has been dead these hundred years. He appears to have been the person, who pulled down the old _____ house, and built up _____ in its stead.

Understanding that certain young ladies, of the family of the owner of _____ House, had been recent visitors, or residents there, I caused application to be made to them - through the medium of a common friend; to the end that if they had "personally-individually or collectively" - been witnesses of the extraordinary noises, I might be favoured, also, with their statements.

And in the careless, confidential, style of correspondence with a near relative - as the said common friend is, of mine - it would appear that in such application and queries, I made use of some such precautionary expressions as the following, touching with reference to the said young ladies; with whom it is not my good fortune to be acquainted: - "if they were steady, sober, young persons, in whose testimony - if they would give any - reliance might be safely placed: " - otherwise - "if they had a tendency to hoaxing, or the like," not to apply to them. To which I appear to have added, the haply somewhat impertinent, question – "are they handsome?"

My corresponding kinswoman, in haste, perhaps or inadvertence, instead of putting my application into appropriate respectful language, sent my inquisitive note to _____ House: - and it fell into the hands of the young ladies themselves.

So much seems expedient for the better understanding of certain passages in the returns with which I was favoured, through the same channel, from the ladies in question.

No.30

FIRST YOUNG LADY'S "TESTIMONIAL TO THE GHOST."

Last heard – 6th July in the evening, between ten and eleven, prayer time. First came the thumping, the usual "Ghost" – then like heavy tread, as if Mr _____ who was out, was come in; but he was not. Then rumbling, not easy to describe. No-one has been "individually" haunted – it is always "collectively." I am very handsome; "individually or collectively" we are all very handsome: and I am "steady and sober." I have thought I heard it in the day, and very early in the evening.

No.31

Mr. _____ the visitor who slept in the next room, as before related, in page 93.

The noise that night he firmly attests to: it happened last September, about three a.m

He first thought the noises caused by beetles. * He heard the noise 6th July ; so loud, and so far believed that somebody had entered the hall, that he began to consider whether Mr._____ had a key, and could have let himself in, during prayers.

No.32

SECOND YOUNG LADY, SAYS:-

When I was a little girl nine or ten years old, the nursery maid left me in bed always, to go down to her supper. She once came up, and scolded me, for getting out of bed and making a trampling noise over the kitchen. I had not moved; and afterwards she told me she often heard it, and thought it was I who made it. It has never waked me in the night; but when awake I have often heard the thumps. They always seem to me to be in the kitchen: and I do not think they are heard in the day; and I am very "sober" and very "handsome."

No.33.

ANOTHER SISTER - ALSO A VISTANT AT _____ HOUSE - RECENTLY MARRIED.

There seems no doubt of *my* "sobriety and steadiness." - I therefore, without farther comment, can certainly speak to having heard long and heavy and distant thumpings, very often; in the middle of the night. I differ from other relators in two points. - It always seems to me over my

* Not the insect; it is believed – but the implement – E.M.

bedroom – where a man servant sleeps. It is no noise —made by him. 2. – I believe that I have twice heard the same sounds in the day-time; though other noises have prevented my being clear about it. They say it is very loud every night this week.

While prosecuting the enquiries touching on the mysterious sounds at _____House, I learned that my nephew, Captain Frazer, of the Royal Artillery, had been a visitor there; and had, in common with the family, and others, heard them.

I, therefore, requested him to favour me with a relation of what he had heard, and thought, referring thereto. And in reply, I received the following communication:

No.34

CARLISLE, 19th *July*, 1841.

With regard to the "Haunted House" affair, at _____ House, I will give as full and minute an account as I can. I wrote an account at the time; which has been unfortunately destroyed; but as the facts are well impressed on my memory, the loss of it is of less consequence.

Soon after my intimacy with L. began, he invited me to stay, a few days at his mother's house, in _____shire. "You must know," he laughingly added, "that our's is a haunted house, and has been so for many years. The inconvenience of this reputation has been very great; as, at times, we have had difficulty in getting servants to stay with us; especially maid-servants: and we have by common consent, dropped all allusion to the subject; and I now mention it to you that you may not, during your visit, transgress this rule."

"About twenty years ago" (I think he said twenty) "when we first came to ——House, there was an old house adjoining it; in which a bailiff, who had charge of the estate, lived with his family. Very strange noises used to be heard after eleven o'clock almost every night; which we attributed at first to the people in the other house; and did not, in consequence, pay so much attention to them as we afterwards did. But when the bailiff left this house (which we intended pulling down) we asked him why he had every night made such a noise ? To our great surprise, he informed us, that he was not the occasion of it; and we found both from him, and from other enquiries we set on foot, that the house had enjoyed the reputation of being haunted for many years. It appeared that some of the oldest inhabitants of the village, in the parish, that _____ House had formerly been occupied by an eccentric and dubious character, yclept 'Squire _____ . This gentleman had in his younger days travelled much on the continent; and had, amongst other countries, visited Italy; and brought home with him on his return to England, an Italian valet – also a character. The two lived in seclusion at _____ House; and in process of time many reports and suspicions got abroad respecting them, and the doings at the hall : though nothing definitive could be brought against 'Squire _____ : except his being a great miser. At last he died, or disappeared "(I forget which L. said)" and shortly afterwards noises began to be heard in the house; and the common legend was, that he had been *bricked up* by his Italian servant, between the walls in some room or vault, and so left to perish; and that the noise was occasioned by his rapping the walls with the butt end of his hunting whip, in trying to get out."

Such was L.'s account. He added other particulars; which, as you have probably had them from some of the family, in a more authentic form than I could give them, I omit. Now for my own part in the mystery. As I had never before been in a haunted house, my curiosity was greatly excited; and I persuaded L. to come and sit up with me in my bed-room. He did so. The noise began much later than usual that evening; - at least we did not hear about it till about half-past twelve p.m. or quarter before one a.m. It was if some one was striking the walls with a hammer, or mallet, muffled in flannel. It began at *first* slowly; with a distinct interval between each blow; then became more rapid - but afterwards followed no rule; but was slow or rapid, as caprice dictated. The noise did not appear to come always from the same part of the house. Sometimes it was heard faintly, as if at a distance: at others, it became startlingly near; but seemed always *below* the room we were in. It was much louder than I expected. I think if I had been outside the house I should have heard it. I passed three other days at _____ House; and heard the same noise two nights out of three. When all was still and asleep, there was something uncomfortable - not to say fearful - in hearing this hollow muffled noise; moving about the house; and coming at times, so near, that I expected to see the door open, and some person to come in; though no footsteps were ever heard. It usually began about eleven or half-past eleven p.m. But one evening I heard it a quarter-before ten p.m. before any of the family had gone up stairs. The noise generally continued, with intervals, for about two hours; and I think there was a slight interval between every *five* blows; but I am not sure on this point. I never heard it during the day: though when every member of the family was out and all was quiet, I would listen: nor did I ever hear it except in one instance, above named, before ten p.m.

A slight interval between every *five* blows has been mentioned; but it is not meant that you should infer from this, that there was any regularity in the striking of those five blows. On the contrary, the time was very uncertain, and irregular. It was when the blows followed each other most rapidly, that the noise was loudest. It was *only* at *first* that there was any regularity in the interval between the blows. I tried, in vain, to form even a probably conjecture as to the cause of the noise: drains; dropping water; currents of air in chimneys; rats running over loose boards; water-mills, and the falls of water at mill-dams; all suggested themselves. But the want of regularity, in the sound; and above all its locomotive powers, render improbable that any of these should be the real cause. And besides which, they would all be heard in the day-time, if listened for: - but the mysterious sound never has been I believe.

Although always much interested in any thing partaking of the marvellous, I have no faith in superhuman agency in these matters; still it was impossible at night to hear this unreasonable sound, without a slight feeling of depression; and I think, it would have an effect upon a person of weak nerves or mind.

Such is all I can recollect of what I *heard* myself - but the stories were numerous. One night about twelve, the lady of the house was sitting in the drawing room, reading - all the family had retired to rest; when the noise was heard close to a glass door (leading to another room) so loudly, that she got up and went to the spot where it seemed to proceed from;; but nothing of course was seen. There was a strange story connected with the room I slept in: it was told me by my friend L. Many years ago he came home for the holidays from school, and slept the first night there. About the middle of the night, he was awoke by a very loud noise, as if a cart heavily laden with iron bars, was passing slowly along the path under the windows, which were in the front of the house, and looked towards the park. He threw open the shutters and window: it was a bright moon-light night: but he could see nothing, though the noise continued for a short time after. When he mentioned all this next morning he was laughed at for his pains. Some years after this however (I think L. said eleven) an uncle of his slept the first night of his arrival in this very room. When he came to breakfast next morning, in reply to hopes that he had slept well, &c. he said - "it is a curious thing, but I was awoke by a cart, laden as with iron, rattling under my windows; but it was so pitch dark I could not see any thing."

One more observation about this mysterious sound; there are some noises which though very loud, the ear from a long habit of judging of, and weighing them, knows to be at a great distance; but this noise seemed to me (as a general rule) to become loud, or faint, not so much from any change in the intensity of the blows, as from a change of distance and position; and I am borne out in this remark by L. who mentioned that when several members of the family were stationed at different parts of the house, their accounts, as to the loudness of the sound and its distance from them, generally differed.

I have now told you, in a somewhat lengthy style, all I can call to mind on the subject. I thought it better to put down facts as they occurred to me, and leave you, should you deemed them suited to your purpose, to condense* and arrange them as you pleased.

While on these subjects, I cannot help telling you a "Ghost Story," which, though it has no direct connection with haunted houses, is still so different, in time, place, and circumstances, from the received and best authenticated tales of this sort, as to merit some attention; and it has the rare advantage of not having been added to or heightened in colour, by passing through many hands: as I had it from Col. Ed Michell (my old Captain) who heard it from one of the parties, to whom the adventure happened.

One fine September morning, in the year 180~, Lieut. W. and a brother officer, A of the 8 ~ Regiment, then quartered in Ireland, went out for a day's shooting. They were both keen sportsmen; particularly A. who had with him on this occasion, a black pointer bitch - a great favourite: and who seldom or never left her master's side. They were both in high spirits; to which the freshness of the morning air, and the anticipation of a day's good sport had added. As it wanted some little time to day-break, they sat down under a hedge, in a large field, at some distance from their quarters, to watch if any game should pass: and to arrange their plans for the day. Though the sun had not yet risen every thing was distinctly seen in the grey and increasing light of the morning; and the busy hum about them indicated that the active bustle of the day had begun. They had not taken up their position very long, before they

---

* I have made no alterations. - E.M.

heard their dog, who had been wandering about the field (as they supposed) on the opposite side of it; and saw her coming towards them with her tail between her legs, and shewing every symptom of terror. As they could see nothing; but fancied it might be a man or an animal passing bye on the other side of the hedge, they took no further notice of it. The pointer, however, had now crouched between them, and in spite of all their efforts to silence her, kept up a long melancholy whining. Suddenly there shot by them a bright meteor, accompanied by a rushing sound; and this was succeeded by a dazzling light; which together with the noise, went on increasing for a few minutes: when, to their horror and amazement, they saw, slowly advancing, or rather gliding, towards them, in the midst of the light (to use W's own words) "a bloody rider on a bloody horse" – from that part of the field whence the pointer had come, barking. Both were of colossal stature; and seemed as if they had been flayed alive. The apparition passed slowly on about twelve or fourteen feet from the ground; and when just past them, the rider turned his head around, and looked down fiercely on them; and then slowly retired, and vanished from their sight, in a direction opposite to the one he first appeared in. He was about thirty feet distant when opposite to them. The pointer, who had never before been known to leave her master, gave one long howl, and ran off. After W. and his friend had somewhat recovered from the confusion into which this strange incident had thrown them, they looked at each other; each doubting whether he had not been labouring under some delusion; and trying in each other's eyes to read the truth. They then questioned each other as to the facts of the case; and found they agreed in every point.

They tried at first to go on with their sport; and agreed to say nothing to any one about what had happened; but their spirits were too much shaken to enable them to persevere in their pursuit; and they were not sorry that the absence of the pointer gave them an excuse for returning home. The sequel of this story is equally strange and more sad. W's friend A. on getting home, sickened immediately; and died two days afterwards, but not till he had, before several witnesses earnestly attested the truth of the above event.* Some years after this, Michell was quartered with W. at Tarifa, in Spain. They became intimate, and they used to frequently go out shooting together. It was one morning, when sitting at some distance from the fortress, under a hedge of aloes, that W. struck with the coincidence, told Michell the story. Michell describes W. as having been a remarkably gallant, intelligent fellow: very strong minded and of high spirit. He is mentioned by Napier in his History of the Peninsular War: and fell in an affair, soon after the battle of Vittoria. I think you knew Michell.* He was a hard-headed man; not given to high colouring, or exaggeration, on these topics; and you may depend upon the accuracy of *my* account; because I wrote it down an hour after I heard it; and have been copying all this from that writing.

And now, I have, I think, given you a sufficient dish of the marvellous for this time. One more last word, however, about the mysterious noises at _____ House. The weather was changeable, and showery: but there was no high wind, during my stay there: and nothing, in short, to waft a distant sound, and make it appear to be close at hand.

A.H.F

The foregoing plain, unvarnished, tale, received from my nephew, Captain Frazer, R.A. not being so precise as I wished, in regard to the initials of the names of the officers who saw the frightful apparition of the horse and his rider; and year, and number of the regiment being

* I did – and believe him to have been a veracious man.- E.M.

incomplete* – I put some queries to him, and received the following reply:

CARLISLE, 29th July, 1841

Colonel Michell (the name is spelled with a t) *was* "the pleasant, gentlemanly, man" you used to meet, at my father's, &c. I believe him to have been a veracious man – and on these subjects not at all given to exaggeration, as he had a thorough disbelief of anything like ghosts, &c. Michell had forgotten, for the time, the name of the officer who died. It was something like Spigott or Spinett, I think he said. The other officer's named was Welstead, a Lieutenant of the 82nd regiment; - the year was 1808. The passage in Napier, is as follows: - Vol.iv. Chap. V. Siege of Tarifa, 1811. December. "In the night the enemy approached close to the walls, but the next morning Captain Wren again came down from the Catalina; and at the same time, the troops sailed from the convent with a view to discover the position of the French advanced posts. So daring was this sally, that *Mr. Welstead of the 82nd*. Actually pushed into one of their camps, and captured a field piece there." &c. &c.&c.

* Editor's note: The story as related bares a similarity with other experiences involving strange lights in Ireland and abroad, particularly those reported in UFO literature. For example, shortly before Christmas 1910 two men encountered strange lights near Listowel, County Kerry. Suddenly the lights expanded into yellow sheets of light within each of which they saw "a radiant being having human form". (See Evans Wentz, W.Y., *The Fairy Faith in the Celtic Counties*(1911); also cited in Devereux, P in *Earthlights: Towards an Understanding of the UFO Enigma* (1982). The story shares similarities with a UFO incident near Tocrema Farm at Anolaima, Colombia on 4 July 1969 where the closest observer, Arcesio Bermudez, 54, described seeing a figure inside the light. As in this story, Arcesio Bermudez was taken ill soon after the experience and died in hospital with doctors recording mysterious symptoms. (See Murdie, A. "Spirit in the Sky – UFO death in the Andes" in *Fortean Times* July 2002)

Pray observe that it is Michell who speaks all the time, not I. When I first heard the story, my impression was, that Welstead was mentioned by Napier, as having fallen in an affair, before or after Vittoria; and perhaps (as he was killed then) he may be. I never referred to Napier till you begged me: - but I did so in full confidence that I should find Welstead's name somewhere. If this story had been the common one, of "old house," "long corridors," "tapestry," "night," &c. combinations – that, with a fit of the blue-devils, *predispose* people to supernatural appearances, I should not have ventured to have told it you: but can any thing more unromantic and unghost-like imagined, than two subs setting out, in high spirits, across the country, on a bright September morning, in quest of partridges or wild-fowl? Besides, the pointer was a "particeps criminis," if there was any delusion.

Observe too, that there is an undersigned testimony in favour of Welstead in Michell's account. Welstead does not appear to have been a man anxious to tell every one he had "seen a ghost". It was not until after Michell had become intimate with him, that he told the story; and not even then, till the similarity of the situation, on the occasion of the duck shooting at Tarifa, induced him to tell his friend Michell. He had never alluded to it in Michell's presence before; nor did he ever do so again, save once. It was some time afterwards (some months) when pointing to a very large black horse and his rider, both dead and besmeared with dust and blood, he said, "something like that."

A.H. FRAZER

In page 27 it is hinted, in reference to mysterious Bell-ringing, that I had heard something like it, in the "good town of Ipswich; but not the particulars." It was not until after the whole of the preceding matter was in type – and indeed, the succeeding matter also, that I heard any particulars of the Ipswich ringing. In expectation of an authentic communication of many curious circumstances of such event, the press was stopped. But, after, waiting till the last moment – as touching the necessity of conclusion – and not receiving such communication, I am compelled to conclude without it; and to interpolate this, by displacing other matter: - being merely able to add a few particulars with which I was casually made acquainted by one of the eye-witnesses. Had I not expected rather a full and circumstantial account, in time, I should have endeavoured to learn more from my obliging informant.

Some years ago – perhaps seven – a gentleman's family, living at Handford Hall, in Ipswich, were astonished at the sudden and violently ringing of the "shutter-bells" of the room, in which they were sitting. Mr. and Mrs. Aldrich, and, I believe several grown up sons and daughters, composed the family. I am not informed of the exact time of year of this event – nor of the individuals who witnessed what excited so much surprise and astonishment; nor how long it continued. But more than one bell rung, and on more than one evening: and four, at least, most veracious and respectable ladies and gentlemen witnessed it.

Inside "shutter-bells," are not unusual, in town and country. It is well known that they have no wire; but are merely bells, fixed on flexible, bent, thin pieces of iron, about a foot long, if straightened. The end of these pieces are placed firmly into corresponding sockets on the shutters, at night, and removed, when the windows are opened in the morning. Those in question, are described to have vibrated violently; causing a violent ringing, or jangling, of the bells, fixed at the ends of curvatures. Something of this kind occurred in the Derbyshire ringings, as notice in page 57, to a wireless bell, stuck behind the spline of a row of hat-pins.

The highly respectable family at Ipswich – could in no wise account for the very surprising sight and sound, herein be feebly described. I have no room to add more – nor, indeed, more to add: and I regret that pressing time will not admit of my seeking more.

To these very extraordinary and mysterious communications connected with ____House - and "the bloody rider on the bloody horse," arising, incidentally, out of them - I can add nothing. As far as I know they, with the preceding interpolation, will be the closer to this my Collection of "Strange Stories". I have, indeed, an enquiry or two still unanswered. But having arrived at the middle of August 1841, it has become necessary, in reference to the object of this little book, to bring it to its end.

In the absence, therefore of farther mysterious materials, I take my leave, with this

CONCLUSION

Here - and referring to the preceding interspersed remarks - be they of small, or of no, value - I bid the Reader - Farewell: repeating, that I shall hear, with much interest, of any promising attempt to develop the cause of the strange events herein related; and of any farther mysterious "Bell Ringing:" - and shall thankfully receive any authenticated communication of other phenomena of a like nature.

Valedictory verses from first edition 1841

VALEDICTORY VERSES.

Now, Reader, that our Tale is told,
   Canst thou the riddle guess?
Such things, in simpler days of old,
   Were heard with faithfulness.

But we, it seems, are wiser grown;
   Less willing to believe;
And, 'till we see their *Causes* shown,
   Can scarce *Effects* receive.

Too prone all mysteries to scout,
   Which shun touch, ear, and eye;
We search for *arguments*,—to DOUBT,
   For *reasons*—to DENY!—

Out on an unbelieving Age!—
   As on our Course we wend,
How much, on Life's brief pilgrimage,
   We ne'er can comprehend!—

"There are more things in Heaven and Earth,"
   Than the profoundest scheme,
To which Philosophy gives birth,
   Can demonstrate, or "dream!"—

And if these pages serve to show
   A *Truth*, their moral brings,
How much *imperfectly* we know,
   Even *in trivial things;*—

In this a germ of Wisdom dwells,
   Which, might we haply gain,
And profit by—The BEALINGS BELLS,
   Will not have rung in vain!

          BERNARD BARTON.

AFTERWORD
By Alan Murdie

The author of *Bealings Bells* was Major Edward Moor (1771-1848). He was born at Alderton on January 11 1771, the sixth son of John Moor, steward to the Marquis of Hertford. At the age of 12 he became a cadet in the East India Company, arriving at Madras in 1783. At 17 he became a lieutenant and learned native languages. He was twice wounded, first in the assault at Hill Fort in Bangalore and then at the battle of Gadjnoor in 1791 with a musket ball destroying his left elbow. In recognition of his valiant service the East India Company paid his passage back to Britain and his medical expenses. He made a good recovery under Dr James Lynn of Woodbridge and on July 10th 1794 he married Elizabeth Lynn, the daughter of his physician. He returned with his wife to India in 1796, and continued to serve until 1805 when he retired on health grounds, being awarded a special pension for distinguished service. Settling in Suffolk he purchased Great Bealings House - which was to be the scene of the bell ringing - and took up writing. Drawing upon his oriental knowledge, Edward Moor wrote a monumental illustrated study of Hindu mythology entitled the *Hindu Pantheon*. Another substantial work was his *Suffolk Words and Phrases* (1823) which was an extensive dictionary of local dialect words and expressions. Running to over 500 pages it has been called "a quarry of material for the agricultural historian and economist as well as for the dialectologist".[1] Anyone who takes the trouble to examine this detailed and erudite work will realise Moor was a man of considerable intellect and ability well versed in local ways. He also wrote other books based upon his service in India, including *Memoirs of the Early Life of a Field Officer* in 1839 and was a contributor to Naval and Military Magazine under the name "Bandook". He became a member of the Royal Society was also a friend of Edward Fitzgerald the Suffolk poet and translator of *The Rubiyat of Omar Khayyam*.

The Moors had six children, all born in Bombay, only two of whom survived. His son the Rev. Ed. James Moor became Rector of Great Bealings between 1844 and 1886 and his daughter was Charlotte, Lady Hatherley, the wife of William Page Wood, the Lord Chancellor. His wife Elizabeth died on December 13 1835. Moor himself died at the house of his son-in-law on February 26 1848 and was buried at Great Bealings.

Bealings Bells was Edward Moor's last book and as far as is known he did not write on any other psychic topics, although his book *Oriental Fragments* (1835) contains some intriguing local folklore. From statements in the text, *Bealings Bells* was completed in August 1841 and published locally to raise funds for the building of a new church in Woodbridge. It appeared nearly eight years after the principle events concerned, the mysterious outbreak of bell ringing which afflicted Great Bealings House, near Woodbridge in Suffolk. This rather isolated Georgian property occupied by Major Moor and his household was troubled by peals of household bells for which no explanation could be found. Like many poltergeist cases before and since the phenomena were of limited duration lasting some 54 days between Candlemass on February 2nd and March 27th 1834.

On repeatedly experiencing the phenomena Major Moor sent details to the *Ipswich Journal*. His letter is reproduced in *Bealings Bells*. The story seems to have provoked much interest, if not a small sensation, his account being picked up and distorted by other newspapers circulating at the time, to such an extent that Major Moor felt impelled to correct the impression given that he considered the bell ringing to be of supernatural origin - he did not. Nonetheless, the publicity was also to stimulate the publication of similar stories which formed the genesis of the collection of other cases subsequently recorded in *Bealings Bells* and which he prepared for publication in 1841.

In setting out his collection, Moor adopts the technique of describing events in chronological order of his contemporary manuscripts and correspondence, so the details of the Great Bealings case emerge at different places in the first half of the text. Although this may be difficult for the modern reader to follow, the chronological description has the drama of a "live" commentary at certain points, particularly where Moor is describing the bells sounding as he writes. It must be said that his descriptions may seem unnecessarily verbose and "old-fashioned" in many places with excessive use of the semi-colon in the text. However, before the modern reader criticises Moor's style, we should realise that he was a lover of words and languages. We may also remember that readers of today will have grown up in a culture which underwent an enormous reduction in the formality of everyday speech and writing during the 20th century.

The cases described in Bealings Bells fall into an interesting period where belief in witchcraft had declined and spiritualism had not yet emerged. Psychical research itself grew out of attempts to investigate the latter, following the birth of the movement at Hydesville, New York in 1848. However, Major Moor was to die the same year and thus was destined never play a part in the investigation of spiritualist phenomena.

Regrettably we do not know the precise composition of the household at the material time. He talks about his servants and his son and we presume that his wife was also present. The lack of detail as to the precise composition of the household is a factor for which Moor has been subsequently criticised in an attack on the case mounted in 1965 by the sceptical writer Trevor Hall (see below). But back in 1834 there was no poltergeist literature on which to draw and no reason to believe that poltergeist phenomena might be person-centred rather than place centred. It is the relation of these strange events to which Major Moor devotes the first half of the book and which provided the inspiration for him to go on to gather further examples of mysterious bell-ringing. He did so and reproduces the cases he received from correspondents around Britain. These range from the strange ringing of a church clock at Prestbury to what might be termed a poltergeist outbreak at Syderstone Rectory in Norfolk. Other reports came from places as far apart as Westminster, Windsor, Oxford, Derbyshire, Northumberland, Kent and one extraordinary account from Ireland altogether different from the rest in the book and which today's reader may seem more reminiscent of a UFO story.

Major Moor's book has only been subjected to one critical attack in the last 50 years. This came from the pen of the late Trevor Hall in his sceptical book "*New Light on Old Ghosts*"(1965). Trevor Hall was a notorious critic responsible for a series of increasingly vitriolic books denigrating the work and careers of early psychic researchers. He was at his most vehement in his attacks on the character, integrity and work of Harry Price whom he never met but about whom he formed a fixation. Hall's approach was to select an investigator who was deceased and then proceed to attack their research and the character of the investigator on a personal basis. This technique was criticised at the time but did not deter him from repeatedly engaging in it.

This two pronged attack was applied by Hall to Major Moor and *Bealing's Bells*. Firstly he challenged his intellectual status and membership of the Royal Society at the time. Secondly, he attacks Major Moor for failing to investigate the bell ringing properly, with Hall considering that a human trickster lay behind the phenomena.

These criticisms against Major Moor fail to do justice to either his approach or to the period. The fact that the world learns more as it rolls along does not mean it was stupid before. It should be remembered that modern scientific and forensic techniques were only in their infancy (and as regards the investigation of spontaneous cases they largely still are). The practice within a wide range of studies was to send a gentleman of repute to the location concerned. He would conduct an investigation and then report at a later date to colleagues, often through the pages of a journal with a limited and specialist circulation. This approach was applied in fields as varied as botany and church architecture and applied equally in attempts to investigate ghosts and other marvels. (It may be added that this was still very much the approach by the early Society for Psychical Research with the few haunted house cases it investigated such as the Cheltenham Ghost[2] and the alleged haunting of Ballechin House in Scotland[3] although with the added novelty that the investigators of these cases were women).

Furthermore, one should not underestimate the difficulties of pursuing any scientific subject before the advent of modern roads, railways and communications. The fledgling postal service was put to use as were the newspapers. Moor may be subject to retrospective criticism for not giving full details of every person in the household or details about them, about his methodology and its faults in places which will be obvious. But Major Moor can hardly be the subject of criticism for failing to adopt investigative techniques which had yet to be invented.

Making use of only selective quotation from Major Moor's book, Trevor Hall sought to ascribe the bell ringing to an unknown servant girl who was never detected. (He also gave the same theory of the "unknown hoaxer" for a poltergeist at the Epworth Parsonage in 1716). In neither case did any evidence ever materialise of hoaxing and Hall gives no details how such a deceit was accomplished. This omission is particularly interesting in light of the fact that Hall was actually an expert in old conjuring techniques, his doctoral thesis being a study of antique books devoted to conjuring and stage-magic. (Ironically enough he exploited Harry Price's collection of rare conjuring books held by the University of London).[4] Surely, Hall was suitably qualified to explain how such a trick could have been accomplished if it were possible. But he fails to do so.

It seems the prosecuting zeal with which Trevor Hall conducted his attack against Major Moor owed more to techniques absorbed from proceedings he witnessed in the police courts at Leeds where he sat in his capacity of a lay magistrate rather than to scholarly analysis of the case. Elsewhere Hall mentions this judicial role as one of his qualifications for assessing evidence in accumulated in psychical research. Regrettably we do not know whether Leeds magistrates ever acquitted anyone using Hall's novel "unknown trickster" defence in court. Indeed one can but wonder how any bench of magistrates properly directing itself on the evidence would react to a defendant whose only defence to a charge of nuisance or criminal damage would be to claim it must all be the work of some unknown prankster whom no-one ever seems to see or catch!*

As *Bealings Bells* makes clear the fact remains that Hall's suggestion of a human agency was explored extensively at the time, as the correspondence reproduced in the book shows. In refuting the suggestion of trickery, after providing a meticulous description of the lay- out of the bell system Major Moor states:

---

* It may be noted that a book on poltergeists entitled *Sur la Piste de L'Homme Inconnu.Les Phenomenes de Hantise et Possession* ("*On the Search of the Unknown Man*") by a French Police Officer Paul Tizane appeared in 1951 detailing hundreds of cases investigated by the French police between 1928 and 1950 where no human culprit could be detected.

"The bells rang scores of times when no-one was in the passage, or backhouse, or house, or grounds unseen. I have waited in the kitchen, for a repetition of the ringings, with all the servants present - when no-one - hardly "so much as a mouse" - could be in."

Furthermore the bell ringing itself - particularly violent on occasions - could not be duplicated by the simple tugging on the bell pulls even if conducted with force. He rejected other possible culprits including, monkeys, rats and blackbirds. Similarly Moor rejected metallic expansion and atmospheric effects as a cause of the disturbances. Moor's experiments appear to have been particularly thorough:

"Let the reader imagine a person in the passage between the back-house door and the kitchen window, with say a boat hook in his hand - or with a string tied round the five or six parallel wires - and let the person be supposed to pull, as violently as you please, by the hook or string. What would be the consequence ? Not the violent ringing of the five or six bells, whose wires were so pulled. "And why not" - do you ask/ For this reason - to agitate the bells violently, you must pull in the direction of the line of wires, horizontally or perpendicularly - no matter. By your *downward* pull, however violent or gentle, you will in a *contrary* direction: and, if violently, the bells will not ring - if gently they will tinkle gently, as in the usual way of ringing:-but by no means with jerking violence that we witnessed. I have at this moment tried the preceding facts with a hoe"

It would be a mistake to see Edward Moor as an out-of-touch intellectual (or even pseudo-intellectual if one accepted Hall's opinion) alone in an isolated Suffolk property and falling victim to the tricks of local pranksters executed with a peasant cunning). Apart from having had twenty years of military service behind him, Major Moor was well versed in country life and speech and indeed it would be no exaggeration to describe him as an expert on contemporary rural Suffolk life. As mentioned, Moor was the author a lengthy volume devoted to the local Suffolk dialect and anyone who takes the trouble to examine a copy will realise that Moor was well versed in local ways.

Perhaps Commander Gould came closer to the mark:

"If Major Moor and the others were merely the victims of a prolonged and annoying hoax, its perpetrator may at least be congratulated upon having outshone Caligostro – the Davenport Brothers and many mediums of our own day – in that he went to his grave undetected and unexposed" [5]

Certainly, the guarded language which Moor uses and the care he takes to try and authenticate stories hardly suggests the vulnerability of a gullible believer in marvels or one seeking confirmation of a rigid belief system (one can only wish that many modern so-called "ghost hunters" were as rational and thorough!). Although stating his conviction that "no mortal hand" was responsible for ringing the bells, Moor rejects a supernatural explanation behind the bell-ringing. From the outset, Moor was careful to emphasise that he considered the bell ringing as preternatural and not supernatural. Whereas the supernatural was defined as that above the order of nature, the preternatural was that which was differing from what was natural, "Irregular, in a manner different from the common order of nature." (Effectively, this was a forerunner of the term "paranormal" which is used today). Indeed, as regards stories of haunted houses Moor is clearly a sceptic and it may be noted that it his correspondents and not Moor who use the word "ghost". For instance, with regard to his Case No. 26 of reports of phenomena at a property in Windsor he states:

"Haunted House" stories, from the time of the Cock-Lane tricks, to this, have been detected as impostures, or otherwise accounted for: but Bell-ringings have not, as far as I know."

The Bealings Bells case is certainly remarkable in that the phenomena were limited to bell ringing and we do not see any of the wide range of poltergeist effects which have been recorded. There seem to have been no raps or object movements although the bells were moved with a violence that could not be imitated. Harry Price mentioned the bell ringing in other cases (the latter more dubious). The ringing of bells was also a favourite spiritualist performance. Today cases of paranormal door-bell ringing are occasionally reported, and the Rosenheim poltergeist which occurred in Germany in 1967 seemed to have the ability to repeatedly cause surges of power through the telephone system.[6]

However, "one-trick" poltergeists (as they may be termed) are not unique. To a large an extent the poltergeist makes what it can of its environment and some have a predilection for interfering with certain objects and not others, the patterns varying from case to case. There is even some suggestion that poltergeists may be able to increase their range of activities when such phenomena are suggested or discussed by researchers actually present on the affected premises, seemingly as though the poltergeist can respond to what is being said about it. Indeed, possible evidence of this effect may be found in a the letter from Major Moor's son, the Rev. E.J. Moor who wrote to his father saying that at 1.20 p.m. on Saturday, March 22nd the bells had been active when Mr Gurney from the Woodbridge National School was in the kitchen. "Cook had been talking with him on the subject, and he said he should like to hear them." A similar incident is reported at Greenwich on page 73. This apparent phenomena has been given the name "contagion" by John Spencer who described the effect in a lecture at the Ghost Club on March 9th 2001). If so this might explain why the phenomena at Bealings House were limited to one effect. In 1834 there was no general model for poltergeist behaviour to which any English researcher could refer to or from which imitative effects might conceivably arise (assuming the such a phenomena exists) although had Major Moor been a Methodist and familiar with the works of John Wesley, inspiration might have been taken from the Epworth Parsonage account. However, at this distance such ideas are purely speculative and it might just simply be that for whatever reason case the Bealings poltergeist was only interested in ringing the household bells.

Having no knowledge of poltergeists, Major Moor could only speculate as to the cause of the phenomena. Interestingly, he considered that some force of electricity or "galvanism" may have been responsible, an approach curiously well ahead of its time. Indeed, such ideas are still advanced by researchers today who maintain that an unknown aspect of electromagnetism may be responsible for triggering poltergeist outbreaks.[7] Certainly, Moor's approach in terms of examining the phenomena from the perspective of physics rather than any belief in discarnate entities was to prove premature, for after 1847 the spiritualist hypothesis and attempts to prove "survival" dominated psychic research to the point of obsession. In the early Victorian era, the principles of electricity and magnetism seemed very mysterious forces to scientists and lay people alike. Now that they are better understood and familiar aspects of life, psychical researchers look now to concepts derived from quantum physics or the concept of the fourth dimension as being potentially relevant to the explanation of psychic phenomena. Moor's example may provide a warning against the practice of trying to "explain" one mystery by reference to another, as he himself recognised with his comments on "the substitution of unmeaning words for unknown things: *ignotum per ignotious*" (p.58)

Of particular interest are features in Moor's collection of poltergeist cases which are repeated in poltergeist outbreaks across the world many years later. Even sceptical writers have observed how closely accounts of poltergeist phenomena resemble each other, centuries apart.[8] The accounts of disturbances at Greenwich and Windsor are text book examples of poltergeist disturbances and arguably the fact that these striking similarities are to be found in such an obscure work provides suggestive evidence that a genuinely inexplicable phenomena underlies such stories.

Perhaps the most remarkable of these coincidence may be found by comparing the words of Major Moor with a witness to an alleged poltergeist outbreak in Suffolk one hundred years later at the Bull Hotel in Long Melford. At the Bull one of the principal witnesses was the owner of the hotel Colonel H.C. Dawson who had also served in the Indian Army.

Major Moor wrote:

"I have for many years of my life passed over large arcs of the earth's surface, and have seen the divers tricks of many distant people. If this be one, it surpasses all that I have seen". (*Bealings Bells* p. 27)

This remark may be compared with the view of Colonel Dawson speaking of his experiences in India:

I have seen some strange things out there, men with psychic powers and weird superstitions and I am not easily impressed, but the happenings here have made me think there must be something in these things". [9]

Similarities of this nature both in terms of the phenomena and the perceptions of witnesses suggests that a real if fundamentally inexplicable effect is being observed.

As Major Moor himself considered

"If, within the limited extent of my knowledge and enquiry, so many instances of such things have been heard of; it is not to be doubted but in a wider circle, - say all England - very many others have occurred, not hitherto brought to public notice. Some, possibly, still more extraordinary: and, perhaps, so varying in their phenomena, as might, if collected, throw light on such unaccountable occurrences; and haply, lend a discovery of their cause."

Over 160 years later the Ghost Club hopes that by re-publishing *Bealings Bells,* we can play a small part in realising Major Moor's ambitions. It is our hope that republication may encourage a fresh and open-minded examination of historical poltergeist cases and inspire modern researchers to search for further details about the Great Bealings case and others. It is possible that further contemporary references to both Bealings Bells and other cases may yet be found in archives relating to the localities concerned. For instance, the diary of life in a haunted parsonage prepared by the "Minister at Sydersterne", Norfolk would be a marvellous find if it has perchance survived in some archive or collection. [10]

(1)   Stanley Ellis in his introduction to the 1970 reprint of the work.

(2)   McKenzie, Andrew, *Ghosts and Hauntings* (1982)

(3)   Harper, Charles G. in *Haunted Houses* (1924)

(4) John L. Randall in a lecture to the Ghost Club May 2000. See also: John Randall's article Harry Price: The case for the defence in the Journal of the Society for Psychical Research Vol 64 No 860 July 2001 for an assessment of Hall's attacks on Price.

(5) Gould, R.T. in Enigmas (1929)

(6) See Roll, William G. in *The Poltergeist* (1976)

(7) Budden, A, in *Allergies and Aliens* (1995) and *Electric UFOs* (1998).

(8) See R.C. Finucane in *Apparitions of the Dead: A Cultural History of Ghosts* (1982)

(9) *Suffolk Free Press* February 5th 1948

(10) An account of the Syderstone Phenomena appeared in "Adventures With Phantoms" (1946) by R, Thurston Hopkins, which suggests he saw the diary but no further details are given.

GHOSTS OF THE GHOST CLUB

GHOSTS OF THE GHOST CLUB 2000
"revives the lost art of the ghost story"
Strange Nation
The first classic collection of 35 true stories. Features Is It My Time Now? The Lower House, The Obeah Man, The Shoes and many others The Ghost Club's first foray into print! 35 unpublished, uncollected contemporary true tales.
(ISBN 0-9538662-0-3) £5.99

GHOSTS OF THE GHOST CLUB 2001
28 further extraordinary true life encounters with the paranormal. Features The Motorist's Tale, Mrs Squier's Gift, The Bag Lady, The Black Dog and many others.
(ISBN 09538662-2-X) £7.99

GHOSTS OF THE GHOST CLUB
- AN AUDIO ARCHIVE
A 75 minute CD recording featuring readings of a dozen of the stories from the two Ghosts Of The Ghost Club volumes.
(ISBN 09538662-1-1) £9.99

All titles available form:
The Ghost Club   PO Box 160   St Leonards On Sea   TN38 8WA
Please include an additional £1.50 for P & P.

The Ghost Club

If you require any further information
about the club or its activities
or are interested in joining
please contact:

The Ghost Club
PO Box 160
St Leonards On Sea
TN38 8WA

or alternatively visit our website at
www.ghostclub.org.uk